Lexington to Concord
The Road to Independence in Postcards

Mary L. Martin &
E. Ashley Rooney

4880 Lower Valley Road   Atglen, Pennsylvania 19310

Acknowledgments

The commitment, care, and talent of my husband, D. Peter Lund, played a large role in my undertaking this book and the others preceding it.

I would also like to thank:
Susan Bennett and Carla Fortmann,
    Lexington Historical Society
Eric Carlson, private collector
S. Levi Doran, private collector/researcher

Rev. John Gibbons, private collector
Terrie Wallace, Minute Man National
    Historical Park
Lee Yates, Bedford Historical Society
The Staff of the Cary Memorial Library

Cover
1. *Courtesy of Eric Carlson*
2. *Courtesy of Minute Man National Historical Park Museum Collection: MIMA 43158.*
3. An Amos Dolittle print. *Postcard image courtesy of the Lexington Historical Society.*

Published by Schiffer Publishing Ltd.
4880 Lower Valley Road
Atglen, PA 19310
Phone: (610) 593-1777; Fax: (610) 593-2002
E-mail: Info@schifferbooks.com

For the largest selection of fine reference books on this and related subjects, please visit our web site at
www.schifferbooks.com
We are always looking for people to write books on new and related subjects. If you have an idea for a book please contact us at the above address.

This book may be purchased from the publisher.
Include $3.95 for shipping.
Please try your bookstore first.
You may write for a free catalog.

In Europe, Schiffer books are distributed by
Bushwood Books
6 Marksbury Ave.
Kew Gardens
Surrey TW9 4JF England
Phone: 44 (0) 20 8392-8585; Fax: 44 (0) 20 8392-9876
E-mail: info@bushwoodbooks.co.uk
Website: www.bushwoodbooks.co.uk
Free postage in the U.K., Europe; air mail at cost.

Copyright © 2007 by E. Ashley Rooney & Mary L. Martin
Library of Congress Control Number: 2007925361

Designed by Mark David Bowyer
Type set in Amazone / Korinna BT

ISBN: 978-0-7643-2698-1
Printed in China

Contents

1. That Fateful Day

Since Massachusetts Bay Colony began, there had been war. The European struggles and conflicts spread to New England, and the colonists were called to action. During King Philip's war in 1675, the Suffolk and Middlesex regiments were required to be ready to march on a moment's warning. When the French and Indian War began, raiding parties attacked New England settlements. The colonists knew that war was cruel, bloody, and expensive.

Britain defeated France in the French and Indian War in 1763, and the French threat to the colonies ended. To help pay for its past wars, Britain began to tax its American possessions without consulting them. Colonial protest was widespread.

In the fall of 1774, the provincial Congress of Massachusetts created a Committee of Safety, collected gunpowder and weapons, and revived the old New England training bands. All men between the ages of 16 and 50 were asked to enlist themselves in the militia. Older men were organized into a group called the alarm list. The Provincial Congress also recommended that one quarter of the militia be organized in minute companies ready to march at a moment's notice.

In 1775, citizens of Massachusetts considered themselves British, although they were bitter about the 1770 Boston Massacre and incensed about the repressive taxes imposed by the English Parliament. Angered by the Boston Tea Party, British leaders passed a series of harsh laws and appointed General Thomas Gage to establish order. Through soldiers, tax collectors, and other officials, Britain hoped to regain authority over the "provincials" or "Yankees," who were beginning to rebel against Parliamentary control.

The colonists responded with petitions, protests, and demonstrations. In Massachusetts, John Hancock, Sam Adams, and others clamored for the right to run their own affairs; some patriots even called for independence. The gun was cocked for an historic conflict that would divide English-speaking people one from another and see the birth of an independent America.

CALL TO ARMS—AMERICAN REVOLUTION.

Call to Arms. *Courtesy of S. Levi Doran*

The trigger was pulled at dawn on April 19, 1775, on the Lexington Common. Who fired the first shot is not known; what is known is that a shot was fired – a shot that led to the United States of America. Eight dead Americans were left on the green as the triumphant British marched on to Concord and the battle at the bridge. The first blood had been shed.

These two battles at Lexington and Concord, in Middlesex County, Massachusetts, were the first in the conflict between Britain and its thirteen colonies. April 19, 1775, marked the beginning of the American War for Independence.

The American flag flies 24 hours a day in Lexington in honor of those who died. Millions come annually to visit the historical landmarks and buildings, dating from Colonial and Revolutionary periods, and to marvel at the courage of those armed farmers and tradesmen.

The Battle of Lexington. *Courtesy of S. Levi Doran*

The Battle of Lexington April 19, 1775. Major Pitcairn ordered his soldiers not to fire but to surround and disarm the colonials. Seeing the inequality in numbers, Captain Parker ordered his men to disperse. In the confusion, someone did fire and Pitcairn's soldiers without orders broke ranks and fired at random. Pitcairn rode among them ordering them to stop. By the time the skirmish was over, eight Americans lay dead and nine or ten were wounded. An Amos Doolittle print. *Postcard image courtesy of the Lexington Historical Society*

The Prelude

In the spring of 1775, tensions were high in the Massachusetts Bay Colony. Colonists were clamoring for the right to run their own affairs, some going as far as to call for independence from Britain.

Throughout the winter, the colonists had been preparing for a possible confrontation with the British. They had been hiding arms and supplies, training militia, and organizing their defenses. Some veterans of the French and Indian war served as drill leaders. Their "militia" had little in the way of uniforms or military arms; they were armed citizen soldiers preparing for war.

Minute Men

Towns in the Massachusetts Bay Colony maintained "training bands." Almost all able-bodied men of military age were required to serve. In the fall of 1774, the newly formed Massachusetts Provincial Congress recommended that all men between the ages of sixteen and fifty "enlist." About one quarter of a town's militia should become a minute company whose members underwent additional training and could turn out quickly ("at a minute's notice") for emergencies. These men were known as Minute Men. Although some towns changed their militia organization in response to this recommendation, others – many of whom fought in Battle of Lexington and Concord in 1775 – didn't. Those men who gathered on the Lexington Green on April 19 were part of a single large unit known as a "town training band."

Over time, Minute Men became a generic term for any American militia of the Revolutionary Period.

On April 18, 1775, the military governor of Massachusetts, General Thomas Gage, decided to send British troops under the command of under Lt. Col. Francis Smith and Marine Major John Pitcairn to Concord to destroy the military stores and supplies collected there. Seven hundred British regulars would leave Boston, cross the Charles River at 10 p.m. that night, and arrest Samuel Adams and John Hancock, prominent leaders in the colonial cause, who were purported to be in Lexington. Following their capture, the troops were then to march to Concord and destroy the military supplies stored there. A relief column under the command of Lord Hugh Percy would leave six hours after the main column.

Word of General Gage's intentions reached the patriots, prompting them to sound the alarm. Paul Revere and his cohorts arranged for a signal. Should the British regulars move out by land over Boston Neck, one lantern was to be hung from the steeple of the North Church, Boston's tallest building at that time. If by sea, across the river, two lanterns were to be hung.

One signal lantern now resides at the Concord Museum in Concord, Massachusetts.

Paul Revere's Ride
Henry Wadsworth Longfellow

Listen my children and you shall hear
Of the midnight ride of Paul Revere,
On the eighteenth of April, in Seventy-five;
Hardly a man is now alive
Who remembers that famous day and year.
He said to his friend, "If the British march
By land or sea from the town to-night,
Hang a lantern aloft in the belfry arch
Of the North Church tower as a signal light,--
One if by land, and two if by sea;
And I on the opposite shore will be, …

The Alarm

On the night of April 18, 1775, the British crossed the river (two if by sea) and then waded through the swamps of East Cambridge. Through the dark night, they marched, cold and wet, toward Lexington along what is now Massachusetts Avenue.

As the British were being rowed to the opposite shore, Revere set off for Lexington (a ride of nearly thirteen miles) to warn Hancock and Adams about the British troops. Other couriers, including William Dawes, joined him. They raced to rouse the town leaders and militia commanders throughout the area that night.

Silversmith and patriot Paul Revere is famous for his midnight ride. He warned Samuel Adams and John Hancock about the advancing British troops. *Courtesy of Minute Man National Historical Park Museum Collection: MIMA 13456*

PAUL REVERE WAITING FOR THE SIGNAL FROM THE OLD NORTH CHURCH TOWER   42

Paul Revere crosses the Charles River. *Courtesy of Eric Carlson*

Dawes took one road, avoiding British sentries by falling in with some soldiers. Revere took another. Their mission was to alert the militia along the route. "The regulars are coming out," was their cry. In the riders' wakes, meeting house bells rang, drums beat, and muskets fired—all announcing the approaching danger and calling the local militias to action.

Revere was the first to reach the Rev. Jonas Clarke's house (now known as Hancock Clarke house) in Lexington, a short distance from Buckman Tavern. The house, which still stands with its furnishings, was the home of Lexington patriot and minister, Jonas Clarke, his wife, and children.

Today, the Hancock-Clarke House is open to the public.

As Revere and Dawes headed west to Concord, they met young Dr. Samuel Prescott, who had been courting a young woman in Lexington. A Son of Liberty, he volunteered to rouse the countryside.

On the road near the town of Lincoln, several British officers surrounded the night riders. Prescott and Dawes galloped away, but Revere was captured. Glib of tongue and seemingly unafraid, he warned the British soldiers against staying in the area. As the officers and their prisoner approached Lexington, they heard gunfire and the officers released Revere to walk back to town.

Back at the Hancock-Clark house, Revere found Hancock and Adams still arguing about joining the fight. Just before dawn, Adams and Revere persuaded Hancock to leave Lexington for a precinct of Woburn (today this is the town of Burlington).

PAUL REVERE'S RIDE.

PAUL REVERE ENTERING LEXINGTON APRIL 19,1775

"It was one by the village clock when he galloped into Lexington." —Longfellow.

Today this scene is re-enacted the night preceding Patriot's Day in Lexington.

On the evening of April 18, 1775, Sam Adams, John Hancock, his fiancée, and his aged aunt were visiting the Clarke household. Outside, Sergeant William Munroe stood guard with some Lexington militia. When Revere galloped up, it was midnight. Munroe ordered Revere to be quiet—people were trying to sleep. Revere responded, "You'll have noise enough before long. The regulars are coming out."

Revere delivered his message. Dawes joined him and messengers were dispatched from Lexington to the surrounding communities. After some food and drink, both headed toward Concord. Captain John Parker mustered his men, but then when nothing happened, he dismissed them with instructions to reassemble at the beating of the drum. About half of them went to Buckman Tavern, adjacent to the common.

The Case of the Forgotten Trunk

Early in the morning of April 19, John Hancock's clerk, John Lowell, remembered that he had left Hancock's trunk at Buckman Tavern in the upstairs room. It contained papers that could incriminate many leaders.

Paul Revere and John Lowell returned to Buckman Tavern around 4:30 a.m. As they approached the common, drummer William Diamond was beating out the call to muster. About 50 colonists were lined up facing the meetinghouse, and additional men were quickly joining them on that cold gray April morning.

Revere and Lowell walked through the gathering militia, entered the tavern, and retrieved the trunk. Through the window, they could see scarlet uniforms approaching the common. As more Lexington militia came running out of the tavern, they found the trunk, got it down the narrow stairs, and carried it to safety. After all of Revere's heroics, he was reduced to carrying a box and missing the battle!

Every Patriot's Day, the scenario of the missing trunk is reenacted.

"A Glorious Morning for America"

Lexington was a small farming town of about 800 people. Thanks to its ministers, Old Bishop Hancock and his successor the Rev. Clarke, it was a town that believed passionately in liberty. In fact, the eloquent Rev. Clarke had powerful friends in the Provincial Congress.

Colonial soldiers dressed in their own clothing. Clean-shaven, they had long hair worn straight or pulled back into ponytails or queues beneath large weather-beaten hats with broad, floppy brims. Most towns expected individual solders to supply their own weapons and only armed those who were unable to arm themselves. Although they had a ragtag look about them, these farmers and artisans were ready to use their weapons to defend their homes and their way of life.

The British had approximately 700 select soldiers. They were all precision, glitter, and polish, the most formidable fighting force of the era. There was no way that these exuberant, undisciplined, and untrained colonials could defeat them.

All night, bells rang, dogs barked, candles were lit, muskets were loaded as the colonists prepared for the next day. As the hours passed, some went home.

The belfry bell sounded the alarm in Lexington on April 19, 1775. In 1775, the belfry was on the common behind the large meeting house. It had been moved there from its site on Belfry Hill. In 1910, an exact reproduction was built on the original site.

THE OLD BELFRY -
ERECTED IN 1761 - LEXINGTON, MASS.
ITS BELL RUNG THE ALARM OF APRIL 19th 1775.

Located adjacent to the Lexington Common, Buckman Tavern was built around 1693. Members of Captain Parker's company who gathered here are reputed to have drunk "flip" while they waited for the Regulars to appear.

9

Flip

This drink made with liquor or wine mixed with sugar and egg is shaken or blended until frothy. In Colonial times, a red-hot poker was plunged into the brew just before serving.

Just before dawn, the colonials learned that the British were approaching. Captain Parker aroused young drummer William Diamond to beat the call to arms, and the town's belfry rang out the alarm. As the some seventy militia men lined up in two long lines, the distant sound of marching feet and shouted commands signaled the Redcoats' approach. Soon the British column emerged through the morning fog, and the confrontation that would launch a nation began.

Their scarlet coats shining, their bayonets gleaming, the British regulars marched down the road with practiced precision. In the dank early dawn, they marched on to the common, forcing the militia back. Women and children huddled in the doorways and peered through windows of the several houses surrounding the green.

Captain Parker is believed to have said to his troops, "Stand your ground. Don't fire unless fired upon, but if they mean to have a war let it begin here!"

Sixteen-year-old William Diamond beat the call to arms for the Lexington militia.

Drum Beaten at the Battle of Lexington by William Dimond

Copyright 1905 by the Rotograph Co.

5950 Monument to Captain Parker, Lexington, Mass.

For Our Beloved Friends,

Standing on top of a granite boulder, the 8-foot 6-inch bronze statue known as the Lexington Minute Man represents Captain John Parker, the leader of the Lexington militia. The statue faces the British approach route.

Spurring his horse onto the Green, Major Pitcairn shouted, "Disperse. Lay down your arms, you damned rebels, and disperse." There was a silence, and then Captain Parker commanded his men to back off toward the Bedford Road. Most of his men dispersed.

A single shot was fired, British or American, no one knows who fired it, but with it the American Revolution began.

BATTLE OF LEXINGTON.

Drawn by Earl & engraved by A.Doolittle in 1775
Re-Engraved by A.Doolittle and J.W.Barber in 1832

1. *Major Pitcairn at the head of the Regular Granadiers.* — 2. *The Party who first fired on the Provincials at Lexington.* 3. *Part of the Provincial Company of Lexington.* — 4. *Regular Companies on the road to Concord.* — 5. *The Meeting house.* 6. *The Public Inn.*

The Battle of Lexington.

" Stand your ground, don't fire unless fired upon, but if they mean to have a war let it begin here." — *Captain Parker*

Published by The Metropolitan News Co., Boston.

"THE SHOT THAT WAS HEARD AROUND THE WORLD"

On April 19, 1775, the shot was fired that was heard around the world.

THE BRITISH REGULARS OPEN FIRE ON THE MINUTE MEN AT LEXINGTON, MASSACHUSETTS

2313

The regulars fired several volleys and, then, they charged—bayonets fixed. The battle lasted only for several minutes. When it was over, eight Americans lay dead. Jonas Parker died where he had taken his stand; he was shot down and bayoneted. Robert Munroe, the father of John and Ebenezer Munroe, would have been 63 in several weeks. The others died as they attempted to respond to Pitcairn's order. Young Isaac Muzzy was killed instantly. Jonathan Harrington, Jr., wounded in his chest, stumbled and crawled toward his house. He died in his wife's arms on his doorstep. Samuel Hadley, John Brown, Ashabel Porter, and Caleb Harrington all died in that volley from the regulars. Most of the families in Lexington had lost a relative or a friend in that brief moment.

Ten Americans and one British soldier were wounded. To this day, no one knows who fired the first shot.

The British suffered little. Their piercing fifes and deafening drums piercing the chilly grayness, they fired a salute, gave three loud huzzahs, and resumed their march to Concord. Soon after the British departed, the colonials reappeared, to look after the wounded and the dead. They took children to safety and buried family silver and other valuables.

Later that morning, Captain Parker reassembled the Lexington militia, and they marched off for Concord to the beat of William Diamond's drum. Even some of the wounded set off to meet the enemy again.

Shortly after the first shots, Hancock and Adams left the Woburn parsonage, to which they had fled, for a more distant sanctuary. As they departed, they heard the distant gunfire. Sam Adams, always the propagandist, said, "Oh what a glorious morning for America."

The Town of Lexington later adopted his words as the legend for the town seal.

Built 1729, The Munroe House still stands – a witness to the battle.

The Harrington House still stands today. Nine members of the Harrington family are believed to have responded to the alarm.

NORTH SIDE OF LEXINGTON GREEN, LEXINGTON, MASS.

1231—Harrington House, Lexington, Mass.

The monument in the foreground marks the site of the town meeting house, built in 1692. In 1713, the year Lexington was incorporated, a new meeting house was built. This building held the bodies after the battle. In 1794 it was torn down and replaced.

In "Concord Town"

Just five miles away, Concord was the larger and the richer of the two towns. It too had its meetinghouse and its clapboard homes.

Dr. Samuel Prescott had awakened Concord's town leaders earlier that morning. They mustered their militia, hid or buried most of their gunpowder, arms, and other supplies, and sent a scout east to Lexington. They soon knew that men had died in Lexington and that the situation was critical. Those of military age gathered at Wright Tavern to debate their tactics.

Built in 1747, this low-studded hostelry stood in the center of Concord between the public meetinghouse and the militia training ground. In 1774, 300 delegates from Massachusetts towns, led by John Hancock, assumed the government of the Province of Massachusetts Bay. Provincial Congress committees convened in the tavern while the full Congress met next door in the First Parish Church. This congress passed measures ending tax payments to the crown and organizing a militia force to defy the King by arms if necessary.

Pastor of First Parish Church, Rev. William Emerson pled that the colonials attack the British regulars instead of waiting for reinforcements. His demands were ignored. As the British approached, the militia abandoned the town and retreated across the North Bridge, all the way to Punkatasset Hill, which overlooks the town. From this vantage point, they could watch the regulars enter Concord. Militia from neighboring towns in the west joined them.

Later that morning, the two British officers, Lieutenant Colonel Smith and Major Pitcairn, established their headquarters in Wright Tavern.

Lieutenant Colonel Smith divided his forces. He sent seven light infantry companies to the North Bridge, one to guard the South Bridge, and deployed the others in town, where they searched for military stores.

The British soldiers, who searched the village for munitions, found little. They went to Colonel Barrett's Farm and mill, where Tory spies had reported that the Minute Men had hidden their supplies. Most of the supplies had been already moved from the farm to other towns. Just before the regulars arrived, Barrett's sons plowed the fields and hid the remaining weapons under the fresh furrows. They also searched for hidden military stores and weapons in Adjutant Joseph Hosmer's house.

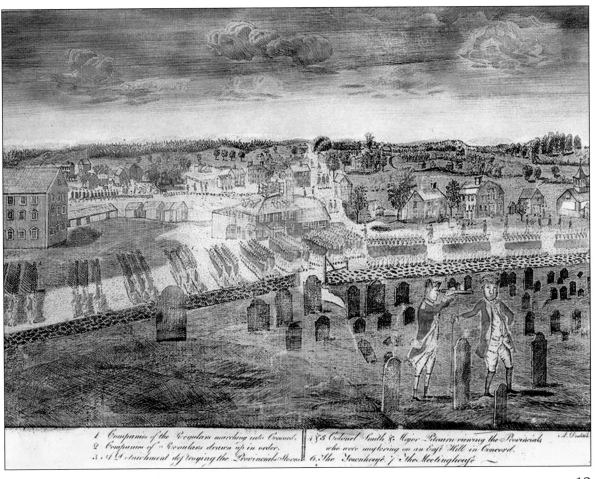

In this view of the Town of Concord, Lt. Colonial Smith and Major Pitcairn, standing in the Old Burial Ground, are looking for the colonial militia who had retreated to Punkatasset Hill. Most of their soldiers were parading in the square, although some are beginning to search adjacent buildings for munitions. An Amos Doolittle print. *Postcard image courtesy of the Lexington Historical Society*

Wright Tavern, with its red clapboards and double-hipped roof, played a major role in Concord's history. It still stands today.

Wright Tavern Built 1747, Concord, Mass.

Rev. William Emerson, Pastor of First Parish Church, garbed for battle.

PARSON EMERSON AT CONCORD.

14

Barrett's Farm.

The Col. James Barrett House, Concord, Mass.

One of the oldest homes in Concord, the Joseph Hosmer House was the home of a well-known cabinet maker and farmer. He probably added the rear portion and gambrel ell c. 1757.

The Hosmer House, Concord, Mass.

To punish the defiant colonists, the regulars chopped down the Concord liberty pole and burned it. They set fire to some wooden gun carriages. The flames spread to the Town House, setting its roof on fire. After the townspeople begged for help, the regulars joined in to form a bucket brigade, which saved the building.

Liberty Pole

A liberty pole is a tall wooden pole, which may be surmounted by an ensign or a liberty cap. The custom of raising and capping a liberty pole goes back to the summer of 1765, when militant Bostonians demonstrated against the Stamp Act. In August, they burned two tax officials in effigy from the limbs of an elm tree. This tree, which soon became known as the Liberty Tree, acted as an assembling point for the Sons of Liberty and other patriots. To call a meeting, they would fasten a pole with a red flag tied to the tree. Angered British soldiers chopped down the original Liberty Tree during the winter of 1775-1776. During the same time, liberty poles began appearing in other towns from Newport, Rhode Island, to New York City, New York.

Concord's liberty pole stood on a ridge overlooking the town and was quickly burned by the British the morning of April 19.

Today, on an early Saturday in April, the Bedford Minute Men Company along with other local Minute Men companies raise a liberty pole capped with a red hat with appropriate music and musket firing.

Meanwhile, several British companies were at North Bridge. To the north, militia from Acton, Bedford, Lincoln, and Concord were gathering. Other men were coming from more distant towns west and north of Concord. More than thirty of today's communities from four Massachusetts counties, Suffolk, Norfolk, Essex, and Middlesex, were involved.

Colonel Barrett, the senior American officer, ordered the colonials into a long line facing the bridge. Then someone noticed smoke from the burning gun carriages in the town. Lieutenant Joseph Hosmer asked, "Will you let them burn the town?"

Concord Mass.

Left to guard North Bridge, Captain Walter Laurie and three companies of soldiers were jammed into a narrow path between stonewalls. Someone fired and the fight was on. When Captain Isaac Davis of Acton and one of his men were killed, Major Buttrick gave the order to fire. As the Americans stepped onto the bridge, the British troops withdrew hastily, leaving three dead and nine wounded. An Amos Doolittle print. *Postcard image courtesy of the Lexington Historical Society*

Plate III. The Engagement at the North Bridge in Concord.

1. The Detachment of the Regulars who fired first on the Provincials at the Bridge   2. The Provincials headed by Colonel Robinson, & Major Buttrick. 3. The Bridge

Emerson's words, "the rude bridge that arch'd the flood," refer to Old North Bridge, which spanned the Concord River, providing colonists with a means of getting to Boston as well as to the center of Concord.

Colonial Barrett ordered the men to load their weapons and advance towards the British regulars at the east end of the narrow North Bridge. They obeyed, marching down the hill to fife music. The British officer ordered his men to pull up the planks of the bridge, but he was too late. The Americans marched onto the bridge.

Major John Buttrick was second in command of the Concord militia. As the militia approached the bridge, a British soldier fired without orders. Others joined him, killing two and wounding several Americans. As his men began to fall, Buttrick is said to have given one of those passionate orders of the day: "Fire, fellow soldiers, for God's sake fire." The colonists killed three regulars and wounded four officers. Despite their scruffy appearance, the colonial militia knew how to use their weapons. The British began to fall back. Suddenly, the British broke ranks, fleeing toward Concord and abandoning their wounded.

"BY THE RUDE BRIDGE"—APRIL 19, 1775.

COPYRIGHT, '09, F. E. TULIPER

An artistic depiction of the scene.

At Old North Bridge, the Americans took an aggressive stance.

MODEL OF THE CONCORD FIGHT APRIL 19, 1775
ANTIQUARIAN SOCIETY MUSEUM, CONCORD, MASSACHUSETTS.

17

87049 PAINTING, BATTLE OF CONCORD BRIDGE, STATE HOUSE, BOSTON, MASS

Battle of Concord Bridge,
Massachusetts State House.
*Courtesy of Minute Man National
Historical Park Museum Collection:
MIMA 136036.*

Battle at Old North Bridge. *Courtesy of Minute Man National Historical Park Museum Collection: 13915.*

HAWTHORN'S OLD MANSE, CONCORD, MASS.

Rev. William Emerson constructed the Old Manse in 1770. From its windows, he viewed the battle at North Bridge.

BULLET HOLE HOUSE, CONCORD, MASS.

Elisha Jones, a Concord Minute Man, was guarding military supplies in his house when the British began their retreat. He accidentally showed himself at the door of the left wing and was promptly fired upon.

All was quiet for several hours. The British companies regrouped at Wright Tavern and even rested (they had been up all night) before they began the long march back to Boston around noon.

The Battle Road

At first, no fighting occurred as the regulars wearily retreated from Concord. The local militia had swelled to about 1,000 men as militia men from Sudbury, Framingham, and other neighboring towns joined the colonials who had fought at the North Bridge. They were spoiling for a fight.

In April 1775, Nathan and Abigail Meriam owned the house, c. 1650-1700, at Meriam's Corner. More than 500 colonial militia had moved across the fields as the British were marching down the road. Just beyond where the road joins Old Bedford Road, a narrow bridge crossed a small brook. The British were jammed together as they crossed the bridge. Suddenly, muskets

fired. That began the rout. For the next sixteen miles of their march back to Boston, the British would be shot at, set upon, harassed, and killed.

Some of the Americans who fought that day had fought in the French and Indian War. Drawing on that experience, the militia set up ambushes from behind stonewalls, rocks, and orchards; they advanced, covered, and retreated. The fighting grew in intensity. Orderly retreat soon turned to a rout. The British took many casualties, while the guerrilla tactics of the locals kept their losses to a minimum.

Yankee Doodle

The origin of the word "Yankee" is unclear, but by the mid-1700s it referred to the English colonists, particularly New Englanders. British military officers sung "Yankee Doodle Dandy" before the Revolution to mock the "Yankees" with whom they served in the French and Indian War. A "dandy" is a British term for a man who spends his income on clothes in order to "appear above his station." A "doodle" was a country bumpkin.

On April 19, 1775, troops under the command of Lord Hugh Percy, played "Yankee Doodle" as they marched from Boston to reinforce the British soldiers already fighting the Americans along the Battle Road. Whether sung or played on that occasion, the tune was martial and intended to deride the colonials:

> *Yankee Doodle came to town,*
> *For to buy a firelock;*
> *We will tar and feather him*
> *And so we will John Hancock.*
> *(CHORUS)*
> *Yankee Doodle, keep it up,*
> *Yankee Doodle Dandy,*
> *Mind the Music and the step,*
> *And with the girls be handy.*

Folklore says that the Yankees began to sing the song as they forced the British back to Boston on April 19, after the battles of Lexington and Concord.

Concord, Mass. Meriams Corner.

During King Philip's War, the house standing at Meriam's Corner had been designated as a garrison house for the protection of the neighboring homes. If an alarm were rung, all settlers would gather there. It is here that the Battle Road begins.

The British column slowly moved through the stone-walled pastures, open meadows, and farmlands. Tired from their long night and hot in their heavy uniforms, they retreated through the afternoon. By the time they reached Hartwell Tavern in Lincoln, they were totally disorganized. On a rocky hillside that is remembered as Parker's Revenge, Captain Parker and his men avenged their fallen comrades in a second clash.

On Fiske Hill, the British column began to come apart. It was there that a regular raised his musket at an American crying "You are a dead man." In turn, he took aim and said, "So are you." Both fired simultaneously. The regular was killed, and the colonial mortally wounded.

The foundations of the Fiske farmhouse still stand here.
An engraved stone slab over the well tells the story.

Grave of the British soldier,
Courtesy of S. Levi Doran

21

Meanwhile, Percy's British force had marched westward from Boston to Lexington with over 1,000 reinforcements to assist Lt. Col. Smith's troops. They established Munroe Tavern, located one mile east of Lexington Common, as their headquarters. During the afternoon, the British soldiers consumed liberal quantities of food and drink and shot at a crippled man whom Sgt. Munroe had left in charge of his tavern while he went off to fight with the Lexington militia. The bullet hole remains in the bar room ceiling.

Built in the early 1690s, the tavern is named for William Munroe, orderly sergeant of Captain Parker's militia company in 1775 and tavern proprietor from 1770 to 1827.

As the British were retreating to Lexington, they saw Percy's brigade to the east. Percy had halted his forces half a mile east of Lexington and had trained two field pieces on the town. The sight of his brigade and the artillery fire that sent a 6-pound ball crashing through the Lexington meeting house was a welcome sight to the Col. Smith's retreating troops. In the foreground we see Percy's brigade attempting to discourage the colonials who are shooting from behind stonewalls. In the background are burning houses. An Amos Doolittle print. *Postcard image courtesy of the Lexington Historical Society*

A Part of Lexington
The Headquarters of Piercy's Brigade.
Fieldpiece pointed at the Lexington Meetinghouse
Burning of the Houses in Lexington.

A. Doolittle. Sculp

Smith's regulars had begun to run, trying to escape the guerrilla-like tactics of the militia. The retreat continued across open land (now Route 95). As they neared Lexington, the British were running out of ammunition and had lost morale and discipline. When the weary regulars reached Lexington, however, they saw Lord Percy and his soldiers with an artillery piece. Lord Percy used his artillery to hold the militia at bay while the wounded were tended to and Smith's men were given a rest.

The British troops continued their retreat through Menotomy (now Arlington, Massachusetts), which the British forces proceeded to plunder and burn. Pursued by patriot militia, Lord Percy's force reached Charlestown that evening, where the cannon on the British man of war *Somerset* offered cover to the Redcoats. They sustained 273 casualties (73 killed; 174 wounded; 26 missing) during the expedition. The Americans suffered 93 casualties (49 killed; 39 wounded; 5 missing).

By the end of day on April 19, the American force had grown to close to 4,000. Once the British regulars reached the safety of Boston on the evening of April 19, 1775, they would not leave again until they evacuated the city a year later. A ring of nearly 6,000 militia and Minute Men turned out to encircle the city, and the Siege of Boston had begun. On April 20, Dr. Joseph Warren set up a headquarters in Cambridge and took control of the political aspects of the events of the previous day. General Artemas Ward took military command of the militia companies surrounding the besieged city.

The Revolutionary War had begun.

Less than a month after the battles of Concord and Lexington, the Second Continental Congress met in Philadelphia, where they voted for independence at any cost. As they were meeting, the British declared that Boston was under martial law. In June, the battles of Breed's and Bunker Hill occurred. It was there that the American General Israel Putnam, needing to conserve ammunition, told his troops, "Don't fire until; you see the white of their eyes." The Americans ran out of ammunition by 5 p.m. The British won the battle but they lost 1,000 men. The Americans lost only 400. Two weeks later, The Continental Congress established a 20,000-man army under Commander-in-Chief, General George Washington.

2. Lexington to Concord and the Battle Road Today

Today, the towns of Lexington and Concord and the National Park Service preserve historic structures and sites from April 19, 1775. During the centennial celebration on April 19, 1875, President U.S. Grant planted a tree on the Lexington Common to commemorate the event. In 1894, the Commonwealth of Massachusetts first observed Patriot's Day as a state holiday. By Act of Congress (1965), the American flag flies 24 hours a day from the 135-foot flag pole in the center of the Battle Green as a tribute to those who stood their ground that fateful morning.

These two New England towns and the road between them have played a major role in the history of the United States and in the world.

The Lexington Battle Green

In 1712, a public meeting decided upon the purchase of the Lexington Common. In 1775, this cow pasture, the center of the community, was strategically located between the road to Concord, the county seat, and the road to Bedford. The town's meetinghouse was located in the triangle of the common facing east. Behind it was the belfry, which had been moved from its original site on the adjacent hill.

Although the battle fought on the Lexington Green began the American Revolution, the residents paid little attention to the green for the next hundred years. In the 1820s, the Lexington Town Meeting voted to fence in the common so it could be rented as a cow pasture. Later, it was used for growing hay, which the Selectmen annually sold to the highest bidder.

Lexington was not prepared for the 100,000 visitors and the turmoil that was created when President Grant and other dignitaries visited during the Centennial Celebration of 1875. Subsequently, Lexington became concerned with preserving the appearance of the Battle Green and surrounding buildings. By 1917, homeowners around the common had signed a covenant limiting their property to residential uses. In 1956, the town established a historic district that includes the common and other historic sites.

Designated a National Historic Landmark in 1962, the triangular green is known as the "Birthplace of American Liberty." It was here that Captain John Parker is reported to have declared to his assembled company of militia, "Stand your ground. Don't fire unless fired upon but if they mean to have war let it begin here." Within minutes, eight patriots fell mortally wounded. Captain Parker is immortalized in a statue on one end of the green.

The Lexington Green has seen young and old lovers, babies and seniors, a battle and its reenactments, receptions for Presidents Grant and Ford and General Lafayette, political protests, rallies, a mass arrest, a memorial to those who died on September 11, baseball, catch, and ultimate Frisbee, and other social activities.

The Lexington Battle Green has several memorials, including the Minuteman, the Revolutionary War monument, and the Parker Boulder.

H.H. Kitson, a Boston sculptor, created the Minute Man statue in 1900 for about $1,853. The bronze statue is an idealized figure of Captain Parker standing on one large stone. A fieldstone water trough stands in front of it. When dedicated on April 19, 1900, it was known as Hayes Memorial Fountain because Francis Hayes had left money to provide a watering place for horses, cattle, cats, dogs, birds, as well as humans. Today, this trough is filled with greenery or flowers. It stands at the point facing towards Boston.

555. CAPTAIN PARKER MONUMENT, LEXINGTON, MASS.

COPYRIGHT 1905 BY METROPOLITAN NEWS CO., BOSTON.

Minute Man.   Lexington, Mass

The Lexington Minute Man.

SITE of

PASTORATES
BENJAMIN ESTABROOK
JOHN HANCOCK
JONAS CLARKE
AVERY WILLIAMS
CHARLES BRIGGS
WM G. SWETT
JASON WHITMAN

SITE OF THE FIRST THREE CHURCHES
ON THE COMMON~ LEXINGTON, MASS.

NORTH SIDE OF LEXINGTON GREEN, LEXINGTON, MASS.

The stone pulpit with a stone Bible, symbolizing the role of the church in the history of the town, is behind the statue. It marks the site of the first three meeting houses. A boulder with a plaque marks the site of the belfry. The flagpole can be seen behind it.

Near the southwest corner of the Green is The Revolutionary War monument to the memory of those who died on the Lexington Common. It was installed on July 4, 1799, on the site of the town's first schoolhouse. Rev. Jonas Clarke's 1799 inscription lists the names of the slain men and asserts the Monument is "sacred to Liberty & the Rights of Mankind!!! The freedom of independence of America sealed and defended with the blood of her sons."

In 1835, the remains of the eight men who were killed on April 19 were transferred from their common grave in Lexington's Old Burying Ground and placed in a tomb at the rear of the monument.

This stately obelisk is said to be the nation's oldest war memorial.

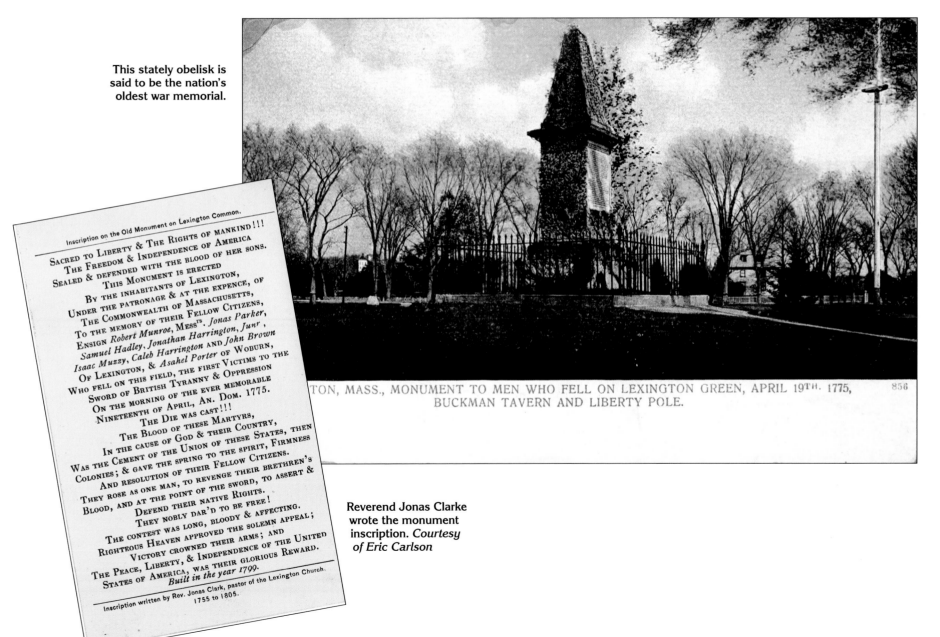

Inscription on the Old Monument on Lexington Common.

SACRED TO LIBERTY & THE RIGHTS OF MANKIND!!!
THE FREEDOM & INDEPENDENCE OF AMERICA
SEALED & DEFENDED WITH THE BLOOD OF HER SONS.
THIS MONUMENT IS ERECTED
BY THE INHABITANTS OF LEXINGTON,
UNDER THE PATRONAGE & AT THE EXPENCE, OF
THE COMMONWEALTH OF MASSACHUSETTS,
TO THE MEMORY OF THEIR FELLOW CITIZENS,
ENSIGN *Robert Munroe*, MESS^rs. *Jonas Parker*,
Samuel Hadley, Jonathan Harrington, Junr,
Isaac Muzzy, Caleb Harrington AND *John Brown*
OF LEXINGTON, & *Asahel Porter* OF WOBURN,
WHO FELL ON THIS FIELD, THE FIRST VICTIMS TO THE
SWORD OF BRITISH TYRANNY & OPPRESSION
ON THE MORNING OF THE EVER MEMORABLE
NINETEENTH OF APRIL, AN. DOM. 1775.
THE DIE WAS CAST!!!
THE BLOOD OF THESE MARTYRS,
IN THE CAUSE OF GOD & THEIR COUNTRY,
WAS THE CEMENT OF THE UNION OF THESE STATES, THEN
COLONIES; & GAVE THE SPRING TO THE SPIRIT, FIRMNESS
AND RESOLUTION OF THEIR FELLOW CITIZENS.
THEY ROSE AS ONE MAN, TO REVENGE THEIR BRETHREN'S
BLOOD, AND AT THE POINT OF THE SWORD, TO ASSERT &
DEFEND THEIR NATIVE RIGHTS.
THEY NOBLY DAR'D TO BE FREE!
THE CONTEST WAS LONG, BLOODY & AFFECTING.
RIGHTEOUS HEAVEN APPROVED THE SOLEMN APPEAL;
VICTORY CROWNED THEIR ARMS; AND
THE PEACE, LIBERTY, & INDEPENDENCE OF THE UNITED
STATES OF AMERICA, WAS THEIR GLORIOUS REWARD.
Built in the year 1799.

Inscription written by Rev. Jonas Clark, pastor of the Lexington Church.
1755 to 1805.

TON, MASS., MONUMENT TO MEN WHO FELL ON LEXINGTON GREEN, APRIL 19TH. 1775, BUCKMAN TAVERN AND LIBERTY POLE. 856

Reverend Jonas Clarke wrote the monument inscription. *Courtesy of Eric Carlson*

The Revolutionary War monument has been at the forefront of historic events in Lexington. It was here that French General Lafayette was welcomed to Lexington in 1824. It was here that World War I solders were bid farewell in 1917 and welcomed home in 1919. It was here that Lexington residents pledged to fight for liberty in World War II in 1942. Ceremonies are held here each Patriot's Day.

Other monuments on the Battle Green include the Parker Boulder, which marks the line of battle established by the Lexington militia the morning of April 19, 1775. The Parker Boulder is decorated with a carved musket and powder horn.

This field piece occupied a place on the green for many years.

Inscribed on the Parker Boulder are Captain Parker's words to his men in 1775: "Stand your ground. Don't fire unless fired upon, but if they mean to have a war let it begin here." Note the gypsy moth collars on the trees. The Harrington House is in the background.

The old belfry. Note the ancient graffiti. *Courtesy of S. Levi Doran*

An inscribed stone pulpit commemorates the site of the first three meetinghouses: "Built 1692, the Parish of Cambridge; built 1713 upon the incorporation of Lexington; built 1794 and burned 1846."

A boulder on the common marks the site of the old belfry, which rang the alarm on April 19, 1775. Just above the green is a reproduction of the old belfry built in 1910 on the original site. Each year on Patriot's Day, children race up the hill in the early dawn to ring the bell.

The Old Burying Ground, with graves dating from 1690, lies west of the green. Most of the stones in the cemetery are slate. The earlier headstones usually have skulls, a Puritan symbol of mortality. Later graves are marked with an urn and/or a weeping willow.

At the rear of the cemetery, a granite marker commemorates Capt. John Parker of the Lexington Minute Men. Towards the north can be found the graves of Rev. John Hancock and Rev. Jonas Clarke, the church ministers throughout almost the entire eighteenth century. A British soldier wounded on the British retreat from Concord on April 19, 1775, who died three days later, at the Buckman Tavern, is also buried here.

Lexington, Mass. From this belfry Paul Revere rang the alarm which assembled the Minute Men, April 19th, 1775. Then located on Battlefield.

To this day, the Lexington belfry rings out the alarm in the early dawn of Patriot's Day. *Courtesy of Eric Carlson*

On Memorial Day, the Lexington Minute Men honor those buried in the Old Burying Ground.

Around the Lexington Battle Green

The Battle Green is still ringed by some of the buildings that were there that morning: The Buckman Tavern, the Jonathan Harrington house, and the Nathan Munroe house.

Facing the Lexington Common on the east, Buckman Tavern, built circa 1710, was a favorite rendezvous for townsfolk and farmers bringing their herds to market and the gathering spot for the militia. After attending services on cold winter Sundays in an unheated meeting house, residents came here for hot flip, a warm fire, and social interaction.

In the early hours of April 19, several dozen Minute Men waited here for the British regulars.

71628 THE BUCKMAN TAVERN, LEXINGTON, MASS. BUILT 1690.

John Buckman owned the tavern during the Revolution. He is said to have given it a new double hip roof to provide more attic bedrooms.

Lexington, Mass., The Buckman Tavern, Built in 1692-Headquarters of Capt. John Parker and his Company the night before the Battle April 19th, 1775.

11401. BUCKMAN TAVERN, LEXINGTON, MASS
July 31-1909. A RENDEZVOUS OF THE MINUTEMEN. A MARK FOR BRITISH BULLETS

It was from Buckman Tavern that Paul Revere saw the arrival of the British. That afternoon, two wounded British soldiers were given first aid here.

In later years the tavern served as the town post office and a store.

Over the years the Buckman Tavern has shown many different faces. Today, it is a mustard color, which is said to be the correct color. *Courtesy of Paul Doherty*

The Lexington Historical Society has restored Buckman Tavern, which it bought in 1913. During this restoration, the workers found the original seven-foot-wide tap room and reinstalled the bar. The restored tap room with its great fireplace has long muskets on the walls, antique jugs, flip mugs, bottles, and loggerheads or heating irons.

USS Lexington CV-2 is affectionately known as "Lady Lex."
Courtesy of Eric Carlson

The tap room in the Buckman Tavern.

A costumed guide tells stories about that time and shows guests the kitchen, ladies' parlor, and landlord's bedroom. Among the many items on display is the old front door, with its bullet hole made by a British musket ball during the battle, and a portrait of John Buckman, the proprietor of the tavern in 1775.

Behind the Buckman Tavern is the U.S.S. Lexington memorial, which commemorates those who served aboard the ships that have been named "Lexington." In 1917, the town asked the Secretary of the Navy to name a new battle ship Lexington. Finally, in 1927, The Navy named an aircraft carrier "Lexington." The World War II monument is adjacent to this memorial.

To the left of the tavern is the Memorial to the Lexington Minute Men of 1775, erected in 1949. It contains the names of the Minute Men who died on the green in the first battle of the Revolutionary War.

The inscription on the Memorial to the Lexington Minutemen of 1775 reads, "These men gave everything dear in life Yea and Life itself in support of the common cause." Bashka Paeff sculpted the bronze bas relief.

The Lexington Visitor Center, operated by the Lexington Chamber of Commerce, is located near the Battle Green and the Buckman Tavern. At the center, you can view a diorama of the Battle of Lexington.

At one end of Lexington Battle Green is a large frame building, which is the Masonic Temple today. The site originally housed the Lexington Academy, a private school, built in 1822. In 1839, Horace Mann, Secretary to the Massachusetts Board of Education, persuaded the state to establish the country's first normal school or teacher's college, and the first normal school in America opened here with three pupils. Frederick Douglass also made his first speech here.

Old Harrington House, Lexington, Mass.

The Harrington house. Every Patriots Day, Jonathan Harrington, wounded by British bullets, drags himself to the doorway of his house facing the Battle Green and dies there at his wife's feet. In 1832, Burr & Chittenden were manufacturing clocks in the house.

HOUSE OF MARRETT AND NATHAN MUNROE--BUILT 1729. LEXINGTON, MASS.

The Munroe house. Nathan Munroe served under Captain Parker.

The Levi Harrington house. This house, also on the Battle Green, was built just before the turn of the nineteenth century.

First Normal School In America, now the Masonic Temple, Lexington, Mass.

The first normal school in America. The school transferred in 1844 to West Newton and, in 1853, from there to Framingham.

Paul Revere galloped down Hancock Street, which is the street to the right.

FIRST NORMAL SCHOOL IN AMERICA—NOW MASONIC TEMPLE, LEXINGTON, MASS.

The west side of Hancock Street, seen above, is occupied by some elegant examples of nineteenth century architecture. Although their styles vary, the fabric of the street is unique.

Other Historic Sites in Lexington

In addition to Buckman Tavern and the Old Train Depot, one of the few remaining shed depots, The Lexington Historical Society maintains Hancock-Clarke House and Munroe Tavern. Both are open for visitors.

The Hancock-Clarke House on Hancock Street is within walking distance of the Battle Green and Buckman Tavern. Built about 1698, the Hancock-Clarke House was the home of the Reverend John Hancock, grandfather of John Hancock, the first signer of the Declaration of Independence and the first Governor of Massachusetts. His successor, Reverend Jonas Clarke, an ardent supporter for American independence, was known for his passionate sermons.

The night of April 18, 1775, John Hancock and Samuel Adams, prominent patriots, were visiting Rev. Clarke in the parsonage. John Hancock's aunt and his fiancée, Dorothy Quincy, were also staying in the house.

That night Boston's Dr. Joseph Warren sent William Dawes and Paul Revere to Lexington with news of the advancing British troops. Arriving separately, they came to warn Hancock and Adams and then set off for Concord. Today, this event is reenacted the night before Patriot's Day.

Hancock-Clark House, Lexington, Mass.
Here John Hancock and Samuel Adams were sleeping when aroused by Paul Revere, April 19, 1775.
Published by The Metropolitan News Co., Boston.

HANCOCK-CLARK HOUSE. LEXINGTON, MASS.

Moved twice since construction, Hancock-Clarke House is now back to its original location, where it stood at an angle facing the Lexington Common. Open to the public, it has a well-tended herb garden.

The Hancock-Clarke house is of particular interest because it contains furnishings and portraits owned by the Hancock and Clarke families and has an exhibit area that includes William Diamond's drum and Major Pitcairn's pistols — treasured relics of April 19.

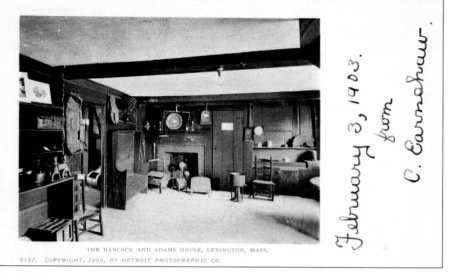

The kitchen

The living room of the Hancock-Clarke House

Hancock and Adams Room   Hancock-Clarke House, Lexington, Mass.

Hancock and Adams Room

Dorothy Quincy Room, showing trundle bed,
Hancock-Clark House, Lexington, Mass.

The Dorothy Quincy Room

A barn behind the Hancock-Clarke House is home to the Lexington Historical Society's Fire Equipment Museum. The Antique Fire Equipment Committee of the Lexington Historical Society was founded in 1961 to preserve Lexington's fire fighting heritage by locating and restoring old equipment and cataloguing historic documents, newspaper articles, old photographs, and relevant memorabilia.

The Munroe Tavern is located one mile east of Lexington Common. Built in the early 1690s, the tavern is named for Sergeant William Munroe of Captain Parker's Minute Man company. Munroe served as tavern proprietor from 1770 to 1827. The tavern continued in operation until the popularity of railroad travel reduced the number of travelers using the road.

During the British retreat from Concord, Lord Earl Percy and his one thousand reinforcements arrived at the tavern that afternoon. Initially, they used the tavern as their headquarters; later they converted the dining room into a field hospital. One soldier shot at the man left in charge; the bullet hole remains in the bar room ceiling.

Today, the building displays furniture and family articles from the late eighteenth century, including the original tavern sign carved from one piece of hard white pine. President Washington dined at the Munroe Tavern when he visited the Lexington Battle Green on November 5, 1789. An upstairs room contains the table at which he sat, documents relating to his trip, and a wooden tricorn hatbox dating from the Revolutionary period. The grounds contain a lovely colonial garden.

Munroe Tavern

71629   THE MUNROE TAVERN, LEXINGTON, MASS.   BUILT 1695

Lexington, Mass. (Munroe Tavern) This room used by Earl Percy as his "Headquarters" April 19th 1775.

Bar Room

Munroe Tavern, Lexington, Mass.

The tap room

Earl Percy Room

Munroe Tavern, Lexington, Mass.

Earl Percy Room

8 MUNROE TAVERN, LEXINGTON, MASS. HEADQUARTERS OF EARL PERCY ON THE 19TH OF APRIL 1775

Washington Room

President Washington visited Munroe Tavern in 1789 during his tour of New England. He ate in this room in the tavern and met with Reverend Jonas Clarke and many of the participants in the battle.

COPYRIGHT LEXINGTON HISTORICAL SOCIETY   80492

6 MUNROE TAVERN, LEXINGTON, MASS.   ROOM WHERE WASHINGTON DINED, NOV. 5TH, 1789.

HALL AT MUNROE TAVERN, LEXINGTON, MASS.

The hall showing the original stairs. The fire buckets hung in the most convenient place so they could be readily available.

A bedroom

7 MUNROE TAVERN, BEDROOM, LEXINGTON, MASS.

The National Heritage Museum is a unique experience for people of every age and interest and a true discovery for anyone fascinated by American history and culture. The museum offers a great exhibit named *Lexington Alarm'd,* which introduces visitors to the residents of colonial Lexington and explores how and why this community functioned as a launch site for the Revolutionary War. This museum also hosts many exciting rotating exhibits.

The museum is the beginning of a two-hour Liberty Ride, a guided, narrated bus tour of Lexington and Concord.

This cannon is near the spot where Percy planted his field piece to cover the British retreat.
Courtesy of Eric Carlson

The Concord River and the North Bridge

The Concord River is only about 15 miles long, but it has figured in history, literature, and many romances.

You can watch the river slipping slowly away beneath you as the sun slowly rises.

The Concord River at Sunrise

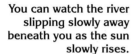

Midsummer, Concord River, Concord, Mass.

The river is a lovely place to be.

When the Lily is in Bloom, Concord River, Concord, Mass.

Old North Bridge, Concord, Mass.

Once associated with a battle, the bridge is now considered sacred ground.

Old North Bridge is where the colonials first successfully resisted the British with force. Visitors can cross the reconstructed bridge and see Daniel Chester French's Minute Man statue.

The Avenue of Pines leading to Old North Bridge in Concord. *Courtesy of Minute Man National Historical Park Museum Collection: MIMA 43148*

236—Avenue of Pines, next to Battle Ground Entrance, Concord, Mass.

THE BATTLE MONUMENT AND OLD NORTH BRIDGE, CONCORD, MASS.

Old Bridge and Minute Men Monument Concord, Mass. (Battle Monument in distance.)

1775
NINETEENTH
OF
APRIL
1875

Old Bridge and Minute Men, Concord, Mass.
Minute Men.   Old Bridge.

The monument and the Minute Man are at either end of the bridge.

Courtesy of Paul Doherty

47

The Town of Concord erected the Concord Battle Monument, a 25 foot granite obelisk, in 1836 to commemorate the first forcible resistance to British repression and the courageous actions of its citizens. When it was dedicated during the town's Fourth of July celebration, the townspeople sang Ralph Waldo Emerson's "Concord Hymn" to the tune of "Old Hundredth."

THE OLD NORTH BRIDGE,
CONCORD, MASS.

The Concord Battle Monument. *Courtesy of Minute Man National Historical Park Museum Collection: MIMA 13536*

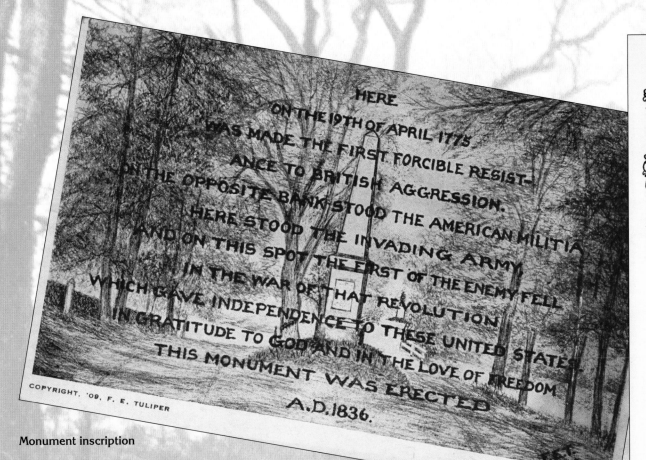

HERE
ON THE 19TH OF APRIL 1775
WAS MADE THE FIRST FORCIBLE RESIST-
ANCE TO BRITISH AGGRESSION.
ON THE OPPOSITE BANK STOOD THE AMERICAN MILITIA
HERE STOOD THE INVADING ARMY,
AND ON THIS SPOT THE FIRST OF THE ENEMY FELL
IN THE WAR OF THAT REVOLUTION
WHICH GAVE INDEPENDENCE TO THESE UNITED STATES.
IN GRATITUDE TO GOD AND IN THE LOVE OF FREEDOM
THIS MONUMENT WAS ERECTED
A.D. 1836.

Monument inscription

CONCORD HYMN

By the rude bridge that arched the flood,
    Their flag to April's breeze unfurled,
Here once the embattled farmers stood
    And fired the shot heard round the world.

The foe long since in silence slept;
    Alike the conqueror silent sleeps;
And Time the ruined bridge has swept
    Down the dark stream which seaward creeps.

On this green bank, by this soft stream,
    We set to-day a votive stone;
That memory may their deed redeem,
    When, like our sires, our sons are gone.

Spirit, that made those heroes dare
    To die, and leave their children free,
Bid Time and Nature gently spare
    The shaft we raise to them and thee.

Emerson.

For the centennial on April 19, 1875, the Town of Concord commissioned Daniel Chester French to create a statue of a Minute Man for approximately $1,000. French's first full-size statue, it stands on a base inscribed with the first verse from Ralph Waldo Emerson's "Concord Hymn." The statue stands west of the bridge.

The Concord Minute Man is both a farmer holding his plow handle and a soldier brandishing his musket.

During the Centennial celebration in 1875, the statue was unveiled. President Ulysses S. Grant and his cabinet attended. Daniel French went on to create the statue of the seated Lincoln at the Lincoln Memorial in Washington D.C.

The bridge also contains a plaque describing the fight on North Bridge and the grave site of two British soldiers.

Two of the monuments near the bridge

Near Colonel Buttrick's farm overlooking the Old North Bridge stands this plaque saying, "On this field the Minute Men and Militia formed before marching down to the fight at the bridge."

Today, this plaque looks over the rolling meadows leading to the bridge.

Wright Tavern. *Courtesy of Minute Man National Historical Park Museum Collection: MIMA 13560*

The North Bridge Visitor Center at Minute Man National Historical Park overlooks the bridge. It offers an exhibit of clothing, uniforms, and accoutrements of colonial militia and British regulars as well as information, ranger programs, and a bookstore.

Major Buttrick Memorial. *Courtesy of Minute Man National Historical Park Museum Collection: MIMA 13534*

The Town of Concord

Built in 1747, Wright Tavern stood in the center of Concord between the public meetinghouse and the militia training ground. On April 19, as the courthouse bell rang the alarm, the Concord militia assembled there. Upon arriving in Concord later that morning, Colonial Smith and Major Pitcairn established their headquarters in the Tavern before the British soldiers' arrival in Concord to seize the colonists' military supplies. Later that day, the British gathered in Wright Tavern to eat, drink, and tend to their wounded after the battle at the bridge. British officers Smith and Pitcairn are said to have waited at Wright Tavern stirring their drinks and vowing to stir Yankee blood that day.

The plaque on the front of the building reads, "Here met the committees of the PROVINCIAL CONGRESS on the eve of the Revolution while the larger body sat in the MEETING HOUSE close by. Headquarters of the Minutemen in the early morning of April 19, 1775. Later that day Headquarters of the British under command of Colonel Smith and Major Pitcairn."

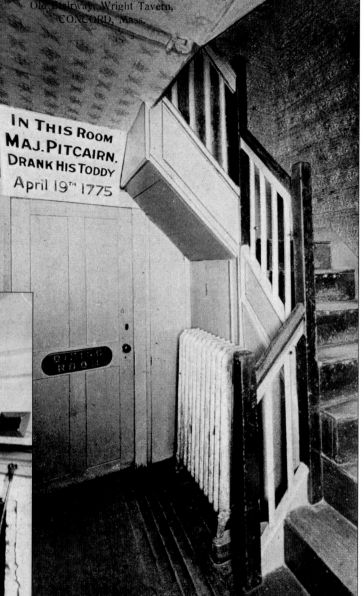

Old Wright Tavern, Concord, Mass.
(Headquarters of British Officers, April 19, 1775. Here Major Pitcairn made his famous boast that he would stir the blood of D — Yankee Rebels before night.)

Interior shots

Interior shot

During the colonial era, the business district was clustered at the base of Concord's Lexington Road, the major road from the east. The British took this route on April 19. Several privately owned clapboard houses from that time still stand on the road's edge.

The Minot House, built 1760, Concord, Mass.

Along with two nineteenth century buildings, the Minot House became part of the Colonial Inn in the late 1800s.

Bullet Hole House, where the hole from a bullet fired during the North Bridge battle, can still be seen.

BULLET HOLE HOUSE, CONCORD, MASS.

The Pellett-Barrett House, one of the oldest houses in Concord, has a stucco façade. It is also known as the Old Chapter House because it once belonged to the Daughters of the American Revolution.

During the first winter, the Concord settlers built homes on the southern slope of a hill in the center of town. They established their meeting house on the hill and buried their dead nearby in The Old Hill Burying Ground. It contains the graves of Reverend William Emerson, Colonel James Barrett, Major John Buttrick, and slave Jay John who was allowed to buy his freedom.

The Old Hill Burying Ground dates from the 1600s. *Courtesy of Minute Man National Historical Park Museum Collection: MIMA 13926*

Living Room, D. A. R. Chapter House, Concord, Mass.
Copyright, 1909, by C. B. Webster & Co., Boston.

Courtesy of Minute Man National Historical Park Museum Collection: MIMA 33137

Old Burying Ground and Unitarian Church, Concord, M

It contains the graves of colonial families and
Revolutionary War soldiers.

The Old Powder House

Concord, Mass., Old Powder House.

Concord, Mass., Tablet to John Jack.

John Jack was a former slave who had been owned by shoe-
maker Benjamin Barron of Concord. Jack was able to buy his
freedom before his death on March 17, 1773. A local Tory attor-
ney wrote his epitaph, which concludes, "God wishes us free,
man wills us slaves. God's will be done. Here lies the body of
John Jack." *Courtesy of Minute Man National Historical Park
Museum Collection: MIMA 13635*

Battle Road Trail, Minute Man National Historical Park

The Battle Road Trail follows the original route of the April 19, 1775, British retreat back (east) to Boston. This stretch of historic houses and landscapes, restored to their eighteenth century appearance, parallels Route 2A in Lexington, Lincoln, and Concord and Lexington Road in Concord. Highlights include the Bloody Curve or Angle where the Battle Road made sharp turns providing ambush points for the colonists, the site of Paul Revere's capture during his famous ride, the restored eighteenth century house of Captain William Smith of the Lincoln Minute Men, and the Ephraim Hartwell Tavern (now an interpretive site) where travelers were offered bed and board.

Today, Meriam's Corner marks the western end of the recreated Battle Road Trail. Less than a mile west from the Concord-Lincoln line and surrounded by meadows, the house stands on what is now Route 2A.

The next main site along the road is the Hartwell Tavern, once a prosperous farm and tavern belonging to Ephraim and Elizabeth Hartwell. In pre-revolutionary days, travelers to and from Boston stopped, visited, and talked about what was going on in the world. From the tavern, the Hartwells could see the British soldiers marching to Concord and retreating back to Boston. Another site is the restored Capt. William Smith farmhouse, the home of Captain Smith of the Lincoln Minute Men.

Today, Hartwell Tavern is a "living history" center. Park rangers and volunteers dressed in period clothing demonstrate colonial activities and provide insight into colonial life. *Courtesy of Paul Doherty*

Meriam's Corner

The restored Capt. William Smith farmhouse has a large central chimney in the "10 Commandments" style. The recessed brick in the front face forms two tablets of stone. *Courtesy of Paul Doherty*

WHERE PAUL REVERE WAS CAPTURED

This monument marks the site of Paul Revere's capture.

Further down the road is the Paul Revere Capture Site. After warning the Town of Lexington about the approaching British regulars, Revere and Dawes met Dr. Samuel Prescott, who joined them in raising the alarm. The three men ran into a patrol of mounted British officers. Revere was captured; Dawes escaped back toward Lexington; and Prescott carried the alarm to Concord and beyond. Today, a stone monument and a bronze plaque mark where the famous "Midnight Ride of Paul Revere" came to an end.

The Minute Man Visitor Center in the Minute Man National Historical Park includes informative displays, a forty-foot mural portraying the fighting between Colonists and British regulars, an excellent bookstore, and thirty-minute multimedia presentation "Road to Revolution," which follows the events of that fateful day.

On the western side of Lexington, a colonial and a British soldier met. The latter saw the colonial, lifted his gun, and declared, "You are a dead man." The patriot replied, "So are you." Both fired. The soldier died immediately; the patriot died the next day.

The trail extends 5.5 miles from Meriam's Corner to Fiske Hill in Lexington. Visitors can walk, bike, or even use their wheelchairs through the beautiful fields and restored early American landscape. They can imagine how it must have been that day as the colonials hid behind trees and boulders, firing on the British troops, and forcing them back to Boston under constant fire.

Celebrations

Tourists aren't just a twenty-first century phenomenon. Lexington and Concord have always been popular tourist attractions. In 1776, both Reverend Jonas Clark and Rev. William Emerson preached an anniversary sermon in honor of that day. The former's memorial sermon became an annual tradition for the next several years. Concord also planted a whipping tree!

In 1906-1908, the Lexington and Concord Sightseeing Co. was operating two large sightseeing busses from Boston to Lexington and Concord. *Courtesy of Eric Carlson*

Concord's whipping tree. *Courtesy of Minute Man National Historical Park Museum Collection: MIMA 13937*

The Commonwealth of Massachusetts funded The Revolutionary War Monument in Lexington. In 1792 and again in 1813-14, Concord approached the state legislature about erecting a monument to the battle, but without success.

Many of the earlier celebrations were "small town" events. Lexington held one of its first reenactments in 1822; twenty Revolutionary War veterans were involved. The actor playing Major Pitcairn rode a highly spirited horse considered to be a great actor according to the records of that day.

In 1824, Lafayette visited both towns as part of his trip through the United States. Concord held its reception in a tent on the common, which had room only for town officials, the welcoming committee, a few veterans, and those coping with refreshments. Everyone else was relegated to remain behind the ropes. Tempers rose. In Lexington, an arch welcomed Lafayette to "the Birthplace of American Liberty." School children and fourteen survivors at the battle were among those present.

On the sixtieth anniversary (1835), Lexington citizens took the remains of those who had died on Lexington Common from the Old Burying Ground, placed them in a lead-lined box enclosed in mahogany sarcophagus, and, escorted by survivors, military companies, and distinguished guests, carried them to the meetinghouse, where appropriate ceremonies were held. Then they were placed in a stone vault at the rear of the Revolutionary War Monument on the Lexington Green.

In 1860, as the country was on the brink of civil war, Henry Wadsworth Longfellow wrote "Paul Revere's Ride," which created a national hero just when the country needed one. His record was not quite accurate, however. Revere did not go to every Middlesex village and farm; he never made it to Concord; and if his name had not rhymed with "hear" he might not be so well known! Today, visitors to Boston can visit Revere's house and follow in Revere's footsteps, as outlined by Longfellow, as they walk along the Freedom Trail.

In 1875, thanks to their long-standing dispute about which town was the birthplace of American liberty, both Lexington and Concord began to plan for the centennial. Their celebration would be the first in a series, culminating with the commemoration of the adoption of the Declaration of Independence, to be held on July 4, 1876.

Of the two farming communities, Lexington was the smaller and situated closer to Boston. Although the Lexington Centennial Committee invited Concord to join in celebration as they had for the seventy-fifth anniversary. Concord Town Meeting voted against it. The result was competing celebrations with statues commissioned for the occasion, banquets, and celebrities. Despite the cold weather, President Grant, various cabinet secretaries, and many officials from the Commonwealth attended both.

To celebrate the occasion, Concord built an ornate cedar centennial bridge with two arbor seating areas. They unveiled French's statue of a Minute Man who left his plow to grab his gun. A religious service at the First Parish on Sunday preceded the formal ceremonies on April 19. Despite considerable advance planning, Concord was unprepared for the influx of 50,000 people turning out for the celebration on a 22° F day. In the midst of speeches that morning, the platform holding the dignitaries collapsed, depositing President Grant and others on the ground.

OLD NORTH BRIDGE, CONCORD, MASS.

The Centennial Bridge

Lexington, Mass. Battlefield - Showing Liberty Pole and Elm planted by Gen. U.S. Grant, April 19th, 1875. On the Right the first Normal School erected in America

Later that day, President Grant planted an elm, which can be seen just behind the pulpit. It died early in the twentieth century.

At the ceremony's end, the President, Vice President, and other dignitaries left for Lexington. Meanwhile, the 4,000 guests had a chilly dinner under the tent while the remaining crowds foraged for food throughout the town. By 6 p.m., most of the crowd had gone home, and Concord residents who had invitations enjoyed the Grand Ball in the Middlesex Agricultural Society hall.

On April 18, Lexington held its church service and dedicated the statues of John Hancock and Samuel Adams now standing in Cary Memorial Hall. Despite the unseasonably cold weather, large numbers of visitors strolled the streets, visiting historic spots, and even attending the church services. The crowds increased all day. On April 19, the ceremony commenced at a sunrise with a one hundred-gun salute. Traffic increased steadily; trains with their locomotives gaily decked in bunting steamed into Lexington, depositing even more visitors. The ensuing traffic jam was so immense that rail and highway vehicles finally stopped. One hundred thousand people came to the Lexington festivities.

After the morning ceremonies, a procession was to be formed, which would be reviewed by President Grant. Meanwhile, no train had passed between Lexington and Concord since the early morning hours. The President and his cabinet and some other dignitaries took a carriage from Concord but were stuck in traffic west of Lexington. Many of the dignitaries had to walk. Learning that the President was stuck in traffic at the other end of town, the red-coated National Lancers rescued him. At the end of the parade, the celebrities went to the dinner tent, which had been stormed by the hungry crowds. Little food remained.

The next years were quieter. Lexington erected the memorial to Captain Parker in 1884. In 1894, Patriot's Day was declared a state holiday. In 1911, actors performed the Battle of Lexington on the common. People thought there were too many dogs and children. These days there are many children, not very many dogs, and lots of cameras.

Captain John Parker still stands guard over the Lexington Common. *Courtesy of Paul Doherty*

THE LEXINGTON WAR CHEST, LEXINGTON, MASS.

Lexington citizens supported the war effort with enlistees, bonds, and a Lexington War Chest located in what is known today as Emery Park. *Courtesy of S. Levi Doran*

On another cold snowy April day in 1925, Lexington celebrated the 150th anniversary. There was a 6 a.m. parade, celebrities such as Vice President Charles Dawes, General Pershing, and Boston's Mayor Curley, and a large-scale military procession. Concord reenacted the battle at the bridge in the bitter cold and snow. The celebrities were there too.

By 1948, crowds attended Patriot's Day in Lexington. In 1969, Maine and Massachusetts designated the third Monday in April as Patriot's Day.

In 1971 in preparation for the Bicentennial, the Lexington Minute Men became established as reenactors. The unique aspect of their effort was that they each did a first person interpretation of someone who fought on the Lexington Green in 1775. During the 1975 Bicentennial, the Minute Men performed the reenactment in front of thousands of spectators and President Ford came to town. The Lexington Minute Men still hold the reenactment every Patriot's Day and demonstrate colonial military tactics on summer weekends and special occasions.

In Bedford, there is a liberty pole capping. In Concord, on the preceding Saturday, reenactors march down the trail towards Hartwell Tavern for tactile demonstrations. On Patriot's Day in Concord, the parade crosses over the bridge and there are more tactile demonstrations.

The major event remains the reenactment of the Battle on Lexington Green. And, each year, Jonathan Harrington dies at his wife's feet on the steps on his home at the head of the green.

The Regulars advance – bayonets fixed. *Courtesy of Paul Doherty*

The Minute Men line up in two long lines as they await the Redcoats. *Courtesy of Paul Doherty*

The battle was quick.
Courtesy of Paul Doherty

Ten Americans and one British soldier were wounded. *Courtesy of Paul Doherty*

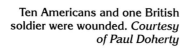

3. Lexington

Lexington grew slowly. In the early years, Cambridge men owned land grants and used the land to farm or just held it. By 1682, about thirty families lived in Lexington, which was then known as Cambridge Farms. In those days, religion was not a choice but an obligation of daily life. The trip back and forth to Cambridge and the long religious services required a full Sunday. Eventually, the Lexington settlers found this too difficult and too expensive, especially during the harsh New England winters. They asked to establish their own town and meeting house.

Cambridge resisted for ten years. Lexington finally gained its independence in 1691 and was formally incorporated under the name of Lexington in 1713.

Lexington built their first meeting house in the fork between the Bedford and the Concord Roads. When Lexington colonists needed more room for a larger meeting house and a school, they purchased "common land," which became known as the Lexington Common. The parsonage, Hancock Clark House, the Old Burying Ground, and Buckman Tavern were nearby.

By 1765, Lexington was a relatively homogeneous community of farmers with similar backgrounds. They grew vegetables, wheat, and flax, kept sheep, and often had a trade to supplement their income. Daniel Harrington, whose house still stands, was a blacksmith, while William Munroe, the owner of the Munroe Tavern, was a cooper. There were some slaves, including Prince Estabrook, who joined the Lexington Militia Company in 1773.

A 1892 Massachusetts Ave., Lexington, Mass.

From Niece Maitha

This postcard, which looks towards the Battle Green, shows the junction of Massachusetts Avenue and Waltham Street from 1892. *Courtesy of S. Levi Doran*

By 1845, the town had about 1,750 citizens who were mainly artisans and farmers. The town was a commercial crossroads with three great roads: Concord and Middlesex Turnpikes and Old Concord Road. Stages and wagons traveled daily through town. Wagons, drawn by oxen and horses, carried produce from Vermont and New Hampshire farms to Boston and returned with cotton, silk, needles, and other luxuries from abroad. Cattle and swine went through Lexington to the Brighton cattle market. Stagecoaches also came through, filling the town's taverns.

East Lexington was more commercially developed than the center of town. It had grist mills and also produced peat, tin ware, and shoes.

The Town of Lexington is about 11 miles north/northwest from Boston and about 12,160 acres or 19 square miles. Its high water table and lack of rivers discouraged mills and industry, but its topography was excellent for hay farming, produce, and orchards. Its milk dealers supplied many Boston homes.

In 1846, the Lexington and West Cambridge Rail Road offered three trains a day from Lexington to Boston. Certain that the train would bring prosperity to town, one of its promoters built a large hotel in the center of town. Initially, the Lexington farmers were the primary users of the railroad.

As the railroad grew in importance during the mid nineteenth century, wealthy Boston residents used it to escape from the city during the heat of summer. Leaving the crowded congested streets, they would enjoy the pastoral scenes and clean air of Lexington, either in their own summer homes or one of the many hotels. Although the Industrial Revolution meant increasing wealth, the Victorians wished their homes to be a haven from the increasingly disease- and crime-ridden cities. City dwellers began to recognize the advantages of family life in a semi-rural environment where the air and water were pristine. Once the railroad became available, a person could hold a well paying job in the city and raise a family far away from urban influences.

In the 1870s, the railroad was extended to Concord. In 1886, the rail route was double tracked; by 1900, 20 trains ran each way —approximately daily— on the Lexington-Boston line. The immediate impact of the popularity of the railroads was the elimination of the stagecoach and drovers traveling through town.

The marked improvement in service resulted in more families moving to the rural environment and the head of household commuting to the city. The railroad commuters developed Meriam Hill in the 1880s. With the extension of the railroad, more residents with new ideas and capabilities moved to town.

By the Sunday preceding April 19, 1900, Lexington and Boston Street Railway began to run public transportation. In the 1910s, hardware, shoe, and food product stores lined Lexington streets. It had several tailors, banks, dairies, piggeries, and farms. Its population was about 5000. In 1910, the police made 162 arrests, many for drunkenness, 1 for bastardy, 1 for gaming on Lord's Day, 13 for spitting on the sidewalk, and 1 for keeping open a shop on the Lord's Day.

Courtesy of S. Levi Doran

The Remains of the Harrington Elm, Lexington, Mass.
About 200 years old. A Witness of the Battle. Crippled by a storm Nov. 1904, down Dec. 1904, and made into Souvenirs.

Cart and horse were still important at the turn of century. This tree was about 200 years old when a November 1904 storm felled it.

The Willows.

THE WILLOWS, EAST LEXINGTON, MASS.

Pub. by L. A. Austin, East Lexington, Mass.

Massachusetts Avenue looking away from the Minute Man. Notice the trolley tracks.

A 1888 Massachusetts Avenue, Lexington, Mass

Cary Memorial Hall commemorates Isaac Harris Cary (1803-1881).

ISAAC HARRIS CAREY MEMORIAL BUILDING, LEXINGTON, MASS. 142

"The Dawn of Liberty," a mural by Henry Sandham, 1886, depicts the confrontation on the Lexington Green. Purchased by the newly formed Lexington Historical Society in 1886, the painting hangs in Cary Memorial Hall between the statues of John Hancock and Samuel Adams, which were dedicated in the centennial celebration. *Courtesy of S. Levi Doran*

Massachusetts Avenue and Waltham Street c. 1915. The horse and buggy are waiting outside – on the wrong side of the road! *Courtesy of Eric Carlson*

Massachusetts Avenue looking towards the Battle Green. The streets were covered with snow in the winter, mud in the spring, and dust in the summer.

MASSACHUSETTS AVENUE, BUSINESS SECTION. LEXINGTON, MASS.

Town Hall, Lexington, Mass.

Dedicated April 19, 1871, town hall was a four-story, mansard roof, brick building. It contained a large auditorium, a free library, a collection of Revolutionary War relics, and a memorial hall. The first floor held statues and tables erected to memory of soldiers who fell in the Revolutionary and Civil Wars. *Courtesy of Eric Carlson*

In 1909, Edison Electric purchased the local electric light company, which had been supplying electricity since 1893. By 1913, the Edison Station was completed. *Courtesy of Eric Carlson*

P6026   Edison Transforming Station, Lexington, Mass.   Photo Underwood & Underwood, N. Y.

Maria Cary's grant to the town was the beginning of the excellent Cary Memorial Library.

CARY MEMORIAL LIBRARY, LEXINGTON, MASS. 147

Lexington is known to have an exceptional public school system. It established its first public school in 1716 – only three years after it was incorporated as a Massachusetts town. In the 1850s, it established its first high school and several more primary schools. Built in 1902, this building was Lexington's high school at that time.

CARY MEMORIAL LIBRARY, LEXINGTON, MASS.

In 1906, the Cary Memorial Library was opened. It was officially named after Maria Cary in honor of her gifts.

Note the stone cannon to the left of the school. It marks the spot where Lord Percy's relief column sited a cannon to slow down the militia pursuing the retreating British.

LEXINGTON HIGH SCHOOL
LEXINGTON, MASS.

After World War II, Lexington experienced significant population growth. The newcomers were predominantly highly educated and interested in education. This high school was built in mid-twentieth century.

Massachusetts Ave., Business District, East Lexington, Mass.

WARDROBE'S PHARMACY

Massachusetts Avenue in East Lexington in the 1950s. Follen Church is on the right.

Religious Life

The church played a dominant role in colonial life. The meeting house was used for both town meetings and church services until the church and town were legally separated in the early nineteenth century. During the mid-1800s, many other religious groups were established in town.

THE HANCOCK CHURCH (CONGREGATIONAL), LEXINGTON, MASS.

Hancock United Church of Christ (Congregational) laid the cornerstone for this building in 1892.

The town meeting house, built in 1692, was originally on the common at the spot where the stone pulpit now stands. In 1713, the year Lexington was incorporated, the town built a new meeting house. This building held the bodies after the battle. In 1794, it was torn down and replaced by a new building. Moved to its current site on Harrington Road in 1847, it is now the First Parish in Lexington (Unitarian Universalist). Reverend John Hancock and Reverend Jonas Clarke were two of its earlier ministers. *Courtesy of Eric Carlson*

Church of Our Redeemer, Episcopal, was gathered in 1885. Today, this building is St. Nicholas Greek Orthodox Church. Redeemer has built a larger church across the street.

The original First Baptist Church was burned in 1891. This building was dedicated in 1893.

First Church of Christ Scientist

The immigration of the Irish in mid-nineteenth century increased the population of Lexington significantly. This increase resulted in the founding of the first Catholic Church, St. Brigid's, in 1875. A new building replaced the old church in 1957.

Birthplace of Theodore Parker, (August 24, 1810 - May 10, 1860) a reform-minded minister of the Unitarian church and a Transcendentalist. Born in Lexington, the youngest child in a large farming family, he was a theologian, abolitionist, and social reformer. His parishioners included Louisa May Alcott, William Lloyd Garrison, Julia Ward Howe, and Elizabeth Cady Stanton. His congregation later grew to 7000 members.

Lexington's Farms

Many moved to Lexington because of its rich agricultural land. The town ranked second in the Commonwealth's milk production in 1875 and was known for its fine produce. By the 1950s, much of the farming land had become residential housing areas.

Lexington was known for its farms. *Courtesy of Eric Carlson*

Garden of Mr. E. S. Payson, Lexington, Mass.

Cutler farm. *Courtesy of S. Levi Doran*

Part of Cutler farm. *Courtesy of S. Levi Doran*

Lexington's Social Scene

The rural town, which was famous for the shot heard around the world, became a dynamic suburban community. Its population increased from 2,270 in 1870 to 3,831 in 1900. Wealthy professionals purchased plots of land and worked directly with architects and builders to create unique homes. Near the center of town and the train depot, Meriam Hill was quickly transformed into a gracious neighborhood of late nineteenth and early twentieth styles. Queen Anne, Shingle, Colonial Revival, Italianate, Greek revival and Richardsonian houses lined the streets.

In 1889, the first automobile appeared in Lexington. The popularity of the train dwindled and it was officially terminated in 1977. In recent years, the Lexington Historical Society has restored the train depot as its headquarters.

By 1890, the Lexington Historical Society had published the first guidebook for the many visitors to the town. The Field and Garden Club dedicated itself to preserving and enhancing treasured town assets: its aesthetics.

Massachusetts Avenue in the late 1940s

MASSACHUSETTS AVENUE, LEXINGTON, MASSACHUSETTS   4472

THE LESLIE HOTEL · LEXINGTON ·

RUSSELL HOUSE · LEXINGTON ·

LEXINGTON DRIVING & ATHLETIC CLUB ·

OLD BELFRY CLUB · LEXINGTON ·

Copyrighted, 1906, Standard Pictures Co., Plymouth, Mass.

Some of the grand hotels

The Russell House living room. At the right of the door is the great mirror extending from the floor to the ceiling, which came from Hayes Castle.

Living Room, Russell House, Lexington, Mass.

76

Old Smoking Room

Old Smoking Room, Russell House, Lexington, Mass.

The Belfry Club was one of the first social clubs in Lexington. Women were even given full membership. Fire destroyed it in 1979.

Lexington has had many philanthropic, social, and political organizations. One of the more exclusive ones was the Old Belfry Club, which encouraged "athletic exercises."

"1775" HOUSE, LEXINGTON, MASSACHUSETTS, ON HISTORIC ROUTE 2

"1775" House

STONEHEAP INN
ANTIQUE SHOP
LEXINGTON, MASS.

Stoneheap Inn housed an antique shop and a tea room.

BLOEMGAARD TEA GARDENS, MONROE STATION, LEXINGTON, MASS.

A tea garden

During the mid-twentieth century, Lexington became known for several of its architecturally unique neighborhoods, which are a dynamic departure from its colonial heritage. Built in the late 1940s by Cambridge's Architects Collaborative, Moon Hill stands as a model of progressive architecture and community buildings. Later, architects Danforth Compton and Walter Pierce developed Peacock Farm, a larger neighborhood of similar contemporary homes. Noteworthy for their natural colors and broad windows, they blend into the surrounding natural environment and share common land. Other architecturally significant neighborhoods are Five Fields and Turning Mill.

The town's Historic District Commission works hard to preserve and protect the historic buildings and landmarks. As a result, the town's colonial appearance has been retained.

Lexington Park

By the beginning of the twentieth century, Lexington Park was on the line of the Lexington and Boston Street Railway Co., where the towns of Lexington and Bedford meet. In 1901, the company took over the park, which had operated as Boardman's Grove in the days of the horse-drawn cars. Advertised as a healthy place, you could supposedly hear the murmur of the pines as you walked on their fallen needles.

Open-sided streetcars from Boston brought hundreds of tourists and people wanting a day's outing. Cars left Arlington Heights, Billerica, and Concord every few minutes. Supposedly, there were twenty-one round-trip trains a day to Lexington Park with its forty-eight acres of walks, velvety lawns, picnic grounds, and pure spring waters, The park offered vaudeville,

opera, or musical comedy every afternoon and evening from June 15 to Labor Day. It had over 3,000 comfortable folding seats.

The park included a zoological garden with rare animals, including buffaloes, zebras, wolves, bears, and exotic birds. It had a Monkey Mansion and an exotic bear pit advertised to be the most modern in the world. It had large floral displays, an electric arcade with thousands of lights entwined in the foliage, a dance pavilion, and a baseball park. The Women's Building had a large covered veranda, a library, cots for children's afternoon naps, and a matron in charge. Mt. Wachusetts was visible from the lookout tower. Dining opportunities included a fine restaurant with private rooms and a casino with confectionaries, temperance drinks, foreign and domestic cigars, and tobacco.

The park operated until the late 1920s. Today, houses cover the land.

The main entrance to Lexington Park was on Bedford Street at the Lexington-Bedford line. *Courtesy of Eric Carlson*

Lexington Park Casino
and Restaurant. *Courtesy
of Eric Carlson*

Benson's Casino,
Lexington Park,
Lexington, Mass.

Main Promenade.
*Courtesy of Eric
Carlson*

Main Promenade, Lexington Park, Lexington, Mass.

Lexington Park Scene

Scene in Lexington Park, Lexington, Mass.,

Capt. Parker Spring and Electric Fountains, Womans Building, Lexington Park

The Captain Parker Spring & Electric Fountain was beautifully lit at dusk. The Woman's Building can be seen in the background. *Courtesy of Eric Carlson*

Woman's Building. *Postcard image courtesy of the Lexington Historical Society*

Siberian camels. *Postcard image courtesy of the Lexington Historical Society*

Feeding camels in Lexington Park. *Courtesy of Eric Carlson*

The zoo had an extensive collection of animals. The bears were very popular.
Courtesy of Eric Carlson

4. Bedford

Carved out of the towns of Billerica and Concord, the Town of Bedford was incorporated in 1729. Both the Concord and the Shawsheen Rivers flowed through this largely forested land area

John Winthrop, the first resident governor of the Massachusetts Bay Company, and his deputy, Thomas Dudley, were given land grants in a place then known as the Shawshin. In January 1638, they went to inspect the area and each chose about one thousand acres. The deputy chose first. Two great stones marked the place where the deputy's land was to begin. The two men called the rocks "The Two Brothers" since they themselves had become brothers through the marriage of their children.

The rocks served as a landmark for the early explorers in the area. In 1894, each stone was engraved with the date 1638.

Two Brothers Rock and the Concord River. The "Winthrop" rock is in the foreground; the "Dudley" in the distance. *Courtesy of Rev. John Gibbons*

In 1728, the seventeen families living in the northeast part of the Town of Concord and the thirteen families living in the southern portion of Billerica requested their mother towns to permit them to establish a town and a meeting house of their own. The expense involved in transporting their families to worship on the Sabbath was becoming prohibitive.

Once permission was granted, they built their meeting house on land in the center of town in 1729. Religious observances and civic meetings were now more convenient. Before the Revolution, the town militia's supplies were stored there.

First Parish in Bedford (Unitarian-Universalist). The second meeting house built in 1817 was used only as a church. It has been modified at the rear several times during the twentieth century. *Courtesy of Rev. John Gibbons*

Because people traveled by foot or by horse, the long travel distances between towns meant that they were quite isolated. The first Bedford minister was Nicholas Bowes, who married Lucy Hancock, daughter of Rev. John Hancock of Lexington. Their daughter moved to Lexington to live with her grandparents and married the young Rev. Jonas Clark of Lexington and April 19, 1775, fame. Nicholas and his Lucy lived in a house on The Great Road known as the Domine Manse, which still stands today.

By 1775, Bedford had many farms and about 470 residents. The town had allotted a portion of its local militia to "minuteman status."

On the morning of April 19, 1775, following the alarm that the British were on the march from Boston, twenty-six Minute Men gathered at Fitch Tavern. Captain Jonathan Wilson looked at his men and said, "It is a cold breakfast, boys, but we'll give the British a hot dinner; we'll have every dog of them before night." The Bedford Minute Men then marched to Concord, joining with the fifty men of the Bedford militia on route. One of the first groups to arrive at North Bridge, they participated in the battle.

Nathaniel Page of the Bedford Minute Men carried the company standard into battle. Many sources consider it to be the oldest American flag still in existence. Designed in England sometime between 1660-1670, it shows the arm of God reaching down from the clouds, with a short sword in a mailed fist on a crimson background. Its Latin motto reads, "Vince aut Morire" (Conquer or Die).

The story is told that after the battle it was brought home and stored in an attic. Originally, it had fringe, but in the early 1800s, one of the women in the household needed to adorn her dress. Hence, no more fringe!

The first minister, Nicholas Bowes and his wife were the first occupants of Domine Manse built in 1733. *Courtesy of Rev. John Gibbons*

Some postcards believe that Minute Men gathered here at the Old Bedford Oak. *Courtesy of Rev. John Gibbons*

THE OLD OAK, BEDFORD, MASS.

Boulder, Wilson Park, Bedford, Mass. Marking
the gathering place of the Minute Men, April 19th, 1775.

Others say that they gathered at Wilson Park, which is the scene of the annual Liberty Pole Capping. *Courtesy of Rev. John Gibbons*

Built about 1710 by Benjamin Kidder, the Fitch Tavern has served as a farmhouse, a tavern from 1766-1808, a school for young ladies, and "an underground railroad" station. Today, it is a private residence. *Courtesy of D. Peter Lund.*

CHAS. O. HODGMAN, . . ARTIST, . . BEDFORD, MASS.

Bedford's Great Road. *Courtesy of Rev. John Gibbons*

THE PARSONAGE, BEDFORD, MASS.

This house was used both by the ministers of the "Church of Christ (Evangelical) and Trinitarian Society" and then the Congregational Church. *Courtesy of Rev. John Gibbons*

The Bedford Flag is on display at the Bedford Free Public Library.
Courtesy of Bedford Historical Society

Bedford's Great Road has many interesting houses built in the early nineteenth century.

In the early nineteenth century, Bedford had a flourishing cottage industry in shoes. A recession put a swift end to it.

During the mid-1800s, the waters of Bedford Springs sparked significant interest. One woman told stories about how the Native Americans had come there to drink and bathe in the water. Later, Bedford residents noticed that their cattle preferred the water from the springs. The water from the three springs was analyzed and found to contain good minerals. People began coming to Bedford to partake of the springs and their curative properties. Hotels were built, and Bedford Springs assumed a spa-like presence.

Sweetwater Hotel. *Courtesy of Rev. John Gibbons*

Bedford House. *Courtesy of Rev. John Gibbons*

Purchasing several hundred acres, Dr. William Richardson Hayden established his N.Y. Pharmaceutical Company in Bedford because of the purity of its water. He developed several original products: Compound Phosphorous Pills, the Uric Acid Softener, and Hayden's Viburnum Compound, which was produced at the rate of 5,000 pounds a year. Enlarging the estate, he developed it into an attractive park and health resort with its own railway connection. Travelers and local residents enjoyed pleasant evenings there.

By 1874, the railroad, running through Bedford, connected Lexington to Concord. The daily trains brought guests to the spa and changes in life-style. The population of Bedford increased to 1000 by 1885. No longer just farmers, the townspeople included bankers, insurance agents, architects, a dentist, and secretaries who commuted to Boston.

In 1900, a streetcar line linked Bedford to Lexington. That same railway company operated Lexington Park, on land located between the two towns.

Bedford remained a small town. Men enjoyed fishing trips, and the town was so pleased with its standpipe that a postcard was made.

Fishing excursion on the Concord River. *Courtesy of Rev. John Gibbons*

Bedford was a quiet town of meadowlands, woodlands, and rivers. *Courtesy of Rev. John Gibbons*

STANDPIPE, BEDFORD WATER SYSTEM, PINE HILL, BEDFORD, MASS.
Elevation of base above sea level, 213 feet; height of standpipe, 100 feet; diameter, 20 feet; capacity 235,000 gallons.

The Bedford standpipe. *Courtesy of Rev. John Gibbons*

Arctic dog sled rumored to be Admiral Byrd practicing before his Antarctic expedition. *Courtesy of Bedford Historical Society*

Before World War II, Massachusetts Governor Saltonstall decided that an auxiliary airfield was needed to relieve Logan Airport, Boston, when it was closed by heavy traffic or low visibility. The state took an area bordered by Concord, Lincoln, Lexington and Bedford by eminent domain and built Lawrence G. Hanscom Field. Route 128 was opened in 1951, and the electronics industry subsequently boomed.

5. Concord

Founded in 1635, the six-mile square Concord is located at the junction of the Concord/Sudbury/Assabet Rivers. Some twenty miles northwest of Boston, the frontier outpost was mainly farmland or woodlot.

Like Lexington, its center was the focus of the town. Concord's first houses ran along what is now known as Route 2A from Monument Square to Meriam's Corner. The Hill Burying Ground, Wright Tavern, and early nineteenth-century houses line the same road that the British marched on April 19, 1775. Among the first settlers were skilled workmen such as carpenters, joiners, and masons.

Even before the Revolution, many Concordians were drawn by the expansion to the west. During the next century, large numbers of immigrants from Ireland, Canada, Norway, and Italy moved to town, but the youth continued to emigrate, and the town grew slowly.

Given the beauty of its meadowlands and the adequate water supply, Concord initially appealed to the farmers. Boston was a hungry market for produce and dairy products. The herds of dairy cattle in Concord began to increase once the railroad connection was made. By 1848, Walden Pond was the home of an ice plant. In the early part of the twentieth century, asparagus and strawberries were important local crops, and a number of farms in area grew fruit trees.

By the fiftieth anniversary of the Battle of the Bridge, Concord had 1,900 inhabitants. Some were tradesmen, some were prospering as farmers because of the growing demand from the urban centers, and some were professionals. There were many shops, hotels and taverns, doctors and lawyers, and a post office. The western part of the town hosted various manufacturing establishments, producing carriages, shoes, bricks, guns, and pencils.

Concord was important in the Commonwealth because it was a county seat. The legal professionals moved into the hotels and inns to try their cases when sessions of the Superior Court were held there. These sessions were an event, and people came to hear the great orators of the day.

Several organizations played a key role in the town's development. One was the Social Circle, which began in 1782, and included most of the men of substance who lived sufficiently close to the center so they could attend Tuesday evening meetings. Limited to twenty-five members, its only program was general, unstructured conversation, but it kept a book of member biographies and discussed new developments in town.

In 1900, Concord's population was less than five thousand. Many family farms, open meadows, and pastures surrounded the town. Residents looked to their own resources for recreation whether it was canoe outings on the river or meadow picnics. Bicycle clubs from Boston clogged the roads on the weekends. The horse and carriage and the electric streetcar were the common transportation.

Nashawtuc Bridge, Over the Concord River, Concord, Mass.

CENTRAL PART OF CONCORD, MASS.

The above is a northern view in the central part of Concord village. Part of the Court-House is seen on the left. Burying-ground Hill (a post of observation to the British Officers in the invasion of 1775) is seen a short distance beyond. The Unitarian Church and Middlesex Hotel are seen on the right.

Concord is unique among early Massachusetts town in that it does not have a common.

Courtesy of Minute Man National Historical Park Museum Collection: MIMA 13638

Main Street today has beautiful examples of colonial and early nineteenth century architecture.

Looking towards Monument Square, which brings all the major streets in Concord together.

Courtesy of Minute Man National Historical Park Museum Collection: MIMA 13974

Civil War monument. *Courtesy of Minute Man National Historical Park Museum Collection: MIMA 13762*

Across from the tree on the right is the site where Mayor Simon Willard and his associates brought "6 Myles of Land Square" from the Native Americans in 1635.

War memorials

MASONIC TEMPLE AND MONUMENT HALL, CONCORD, MASSACHUSETTS   5779

Masonic Temple and Monument Hall

BOSTON POST ROAD, CONCORD MASS,

Boston Post Road

The Tea House. *Courtesy of Minute Man National Historical Park Museum Collection: MIMA 13647*

The Country Store

Concord claims to have had the first public library. *Courtesy of Minute Man National Historical Park Museum Collection: MIMA 13880*

Founded in 1911 as the Deaconess Hospital, Concord's Emerson Hospital was renamed in 1924 after Charles Emerson (a nephew of Ralph Waldo Emerson).

DEACONESS HOSPITAL, CONCORD JUNCTION, MASS.

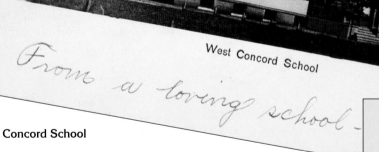

West Concord School

West Concord School

3108. MIDDLESEX SCHOOL, PEABODY HALL, CONCORD, MASS.

Established in 1901, Middlesex School, a co-ed preparatory school, has handsome buildings and well-landscaped grounds.

98

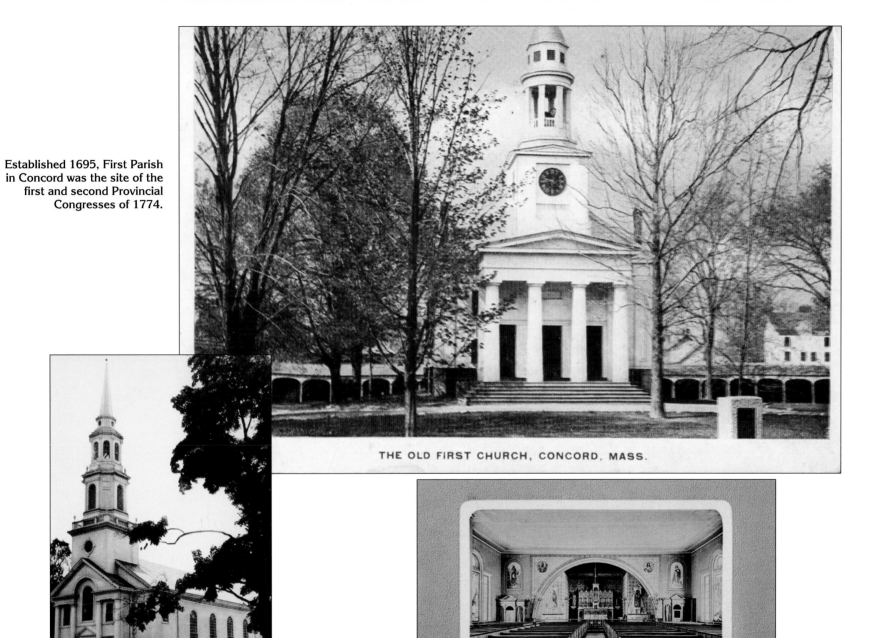

Established 1695, First Parish in Concord was the site of the first and second Provincial Congresses of 1774.

THE OLD FIRST CHURCH, CONCORD, MASS.

CONGREGATIONAL CHURCH, CONCORD, MASSACHUSETTS.

St. Bernard's Church (Catholic) Interior, Concord, Mass.

First Congregational Church

St. Bernard's Church

Colonial Inn

Residence of Store Keeper.   Old Provincial Store during Revolutionary Times.   Residence of Henry D. Thoreau's Grandfather, built by him, 1770.

NOW THE COLONIAL INN, CONCORD, MASS.

The Colonial Inn is at one end of Monument Square.

The earliest part of it was built in 1716. Composed of three old houses joined together, the inn still serves as a meeting place for people from all over the world. *Courtesy of Minute Man National Historical Park Museum Collection: MIMA 13948*

70098 COLONIAL INN, CONCORD, MASS.

The Thoreau family occupied the building on the right while Henry was in college.

COLONIAL INN, CONCORD, MASS.

The original tap room is still intact.

THE COLONIAL INN, CONCORD, MASS.

A dining room

Concord Antiquarian Society

The Concord Museum was formerly known as the Antiquarian Society. Established in 1886, the Concord Antiquarian Society focuses on preserving and promoting local history. In 1887, it purchased the Reuben Brown House on Lexington Road for its collection. In 1930 it moved to a new building at the intersection of Lexington Road and the Cambridge Turnpike. In the first decade of the twentieth century, the society organized its holdings into period room groupings. It has several galleries, period rooms, audio narrations, and hands-on activities to highlight its local history. It also houses some Revolutionary War artifacts, including Paul Revere's lantern.

THE "HALL" OF THE SEVENTEENTH-CENTURY HOUSE
THE CONCORD ANTIQUARIAN SOCIETY, CONCORD, MASSACHUSETTS

CONCORD ANTIQUARIAN SOCIETY BUILDING, CONCORD, MASS

19 OAK PRESS CUPBOARD, AMERICAN SEVENTEENTH CENTURY
THE ANTIQUARIAN SOCIETY, CONCORD, MASSACHUSETTS

ENTRANCE HALL, MID-EIGHTEENTH-CENTURY
CONCORD ANTIQUARIAN SOCIETY, CONCORD, MASSACHUSETTS

10. THE PRE-REVOLUTIONARY ROOM.
THIRD QUARTER OF THE EIGHTEENTH CENTURY.
THE ANTIQUARIAN SOCIETY, CONCORD, MASSACHUSETTS.

KITCHEN IN ANTIQUARIAN HOUSE, CONCORD, MASS.

9. THE BLUE BEDROOM. LAST QUARTER OF THE EIGHTEENTH CENTURY
THE ANTIQUARIAN SOCIETY, CONCORD, MASSACHUSETTS

15. THE YELLOW BEDROOM.   EARLY NINETEENTH CENTURY
THE ANTIQUARIAN SOCIETY, CONCORD, MASSACHUSETTS

27 ROOM IN THE STYLE OF SAMUEL McINTIRE   C. 1810
THE ANTIQUARIAN SOCIETY, CONCORD, MASSACHUSETTS

3. THE REVOLUTIONARY RELIC ROOM.
THE ANTIQUARIAN SOCIETY, CONCORD, MASSACHUSETTS

2. ONE OF THE TWO LANTERNS WHICH SWUNG FROM THE OLD
NORTH TOWER ON THE NIGHT OF APRIL 18, 1775.
THE ANTIQUARIAN SOCIETY, CONCORD, MASSACHUSETTS

Paul Revere's Lantern & Canteen, at
Concord, Mass.

Thinkers/Philosophers/Authors

Concord is famous not only for the battle at North Bridge, but for its philosphers such as Ralph Waldo Emerson, Nathaniel Hawthorne, Henry David Thoreau, Bronson Alcott, Margaret Fuller, and Elizabeth Palmer Peabody. Transcendentalists, they not only shared far-reaching religious views, but also believed in such social reforms as abolition, temperance, and woman suffrage. Then there were authors such as Louisa May Alcott and Harriet Lothrop, better known as Margaret Sidney, who made a significant impact on young women.

Established in 1829, the Concord Lyceum was a source of mental stimulus to these intellectuals. During the winter, it offered a series of lectures. Thoreau gave nineteen, Emerson gave ninety-eight.

The grandson of Reverend William Emerson (Concord minister on April 19, 1775), Ralph Waldo Emerson (1803-1882), left the ministry to pursue a career in writing and public speaking. His basic philosophical faith (one shared by many Americans during that era) is that the ultimate source of truth is within us. He had immense influence on writers and thinkers and became a leader of American Transcendentalism—a New England philosophical movement.

A master stylist, his essays are renowned for the clarity and rhythms of his prose. Among the principles that Emerson addressed in such essays as "Nature," "Self-Reliance," "The American Scholar," and other works are the individual's unity with nature, the sanctity of the individual, and the need for humans to live in the present and trust their own impulses.

Emerson's "Concord Hymn" was sung at the completion of the Battle Monument on July 4, 1837. Considered one of the great orators of the time, Emerson could overwhelm crowds with his deep voice, his enthusiasm, and his respect for the audience.

Ralph Waldo Emerson lived in this square white house from 1835-1882. Emerson's home became a place where students and aspiring writers visited.

Nathaniel Hawthorne and Henry David Thoreau were close associates, and they often walked together. The land on which Thoreau built his cabin on Walden Pond belonged to Emerson. While Thoreau was living at Walden, Emerson provided food and hired Thoreau to perform odd jobs. When Thoreau left Walden after two years, he lived at the Emerson house while Emerson was away on a lecture tour.

Emerson's Study, Concord, Mass.

RALPH WALDO EMERSON
(Daniel Chester French, Sculptor)
CONCORD FREE PUBLIC LIBRARY, CONCORD, MASSACHUSETTS

I am not wiser for my age,
Nor skilful by my grief;
Life loiters at the book's first page,
Ah! could we turn the leaf.
R.W. Emerson.

Concord, Mass. Home of Ralph Waldo Emerson. Essayist and Poet. Born 1803. Died 1882. The "Concord Sage" and Philosopher.

17. THE STUDY OF RALPH WALDO EMERSON
THE ANTIQUARIAN SOCIETY, CONCORD, MASSACHUSETTS

CONCORD ANTIQUARIAN SOCIETY
CONCORD, MASSACHUSETTS
PORTRAIT OF RALPH WALDO EMERSON

Quotes from Ralph Waldo Emerson

It is said to be the age of the first person singular.

Nothing at last is sacred but the integrity of your own mind.

We see the world piece by piece, as the sun, the moon, the animal, the tree; but the whole, of which these are shining parts, is the soul.

A friend might well be reckoned the masterpiece of nature.

It was a high counsel that I once heard given to a young person, "Always do what you are afraid to do."

The greatest homage to truth is to use it.

The Old Manse was home to Hawthorne, Emerson, and early Concord ministers.

Rev. William Emerson, Ralph Waldo Emerson's grandfather, built the Old Manse in 1770. From its windows, he viewed the battle at North Bridge. His successor, Rev. Ezra Ripley, then bought the Manse. When he died, the house was home for some time for Ralph Waldo Emerson.

It is also the house where nineteenth century American novelist and short storywriter Nathaniel Hawthorne lived from 1842-1845, and where he wrote his second collection of short stories, *Mosses from an Old Manse* (1846). After him, Samuel Ripley and his wife Sarah lived there and the property remained within the Ripley family until 1939, when it became the property of the (Massachusetts) Trustees of Reservations.

The Manse has a timeless serenity about it. The view that Hawthorne saw still exists today. Thoreau planted a vegetable garden in 1842 as a wedding gift to the Hawthornes; it still grows in the same location. Eighteenth century stonewalls line the meadows, and the Concord River flows gently past.

14. The Dining Room, The Old Manse, Concord, Mass.

19. The Hawthorne Bedroom, The Old Manse, Concord, Mass.

17. Hawthorne's Study, The Old Manse, Concord, Mass.

Hawthorne's study

Hawthorne's Study, CONCORD, Mass.

President Franklin Pierce stayed there as well as Bronson and Abigail Alcott and their family. Their daughter Louisa May Alcott would become famous in her own right.

The small rooms have been preserved in eighteenth century style with many of the elegant furnishings provided by its famous owners, including a Steinway cross-strung grand piano, eighteenth-century Canton ware, William Emerson's clock, and Nathaniel Hawthorne's writing desk.

Quotes from Nathaniel Hawthorne

Happiness is as a butterfly which, when pursued, is always beyond our grasp, but which if you will sit down quietly, may alight upon you.

A bodily disease may be but a symptom of some ailment in the spiritual past.

No man, for any considerable period, can wear one face to himself and another to the multitude, without finally getting bewildered as to which may be true.

Caresses, expressions of one sort or another, are necessary to the life of the affections as leaves are to the life of a tree. If they are wholly restrained, love will die at the roots.

What other dungeon is so dark as one's own heart! What jailer so inexorable as one's self!

Henry David Thoreau (1817-1862) is closely associated with Concord and Walden Pond on Rt. 126. His *Walden*, a reflection about living with nature, and his essay, "Civil Disobedience," which argues that the individual can resist the government, are still read today. They certainly are studied in school!

In 1845, Thoreau moved to a second-growth forest around the shores of beautiful Walden Pond and lived in a tiny self-built house on land owned by Emerson. The house was not in wilderness but at the edge of town, a short distance from his family home.

Thoreau was an abolitionist, an early environmentalist, and a prolific writer. He worked at his family's pencil factory most of his life. Although he died at age 44, he had major influence on such people as John F. Kennedy, Martin Luther King, Jr., Willa Cather, Ernest Hemingway, Frank Lloyd Wright, and John Muir. Later generations have considered him to be a visionary.

Thoreau lived at Walden Pond from July 1845 to September 1847. A famous example of a kettle hole, Walden Pond was used as a source for ice for export to the Caribbean, Europe, and India.

CONCORD ANTIQUARIAN SOCIETY
CONCORD, MASSACHUSETTS
PORTRAIT OF HENRY D. THOREAU — 1839
ARTIST UNKNOWN

11778. THOREAU'S COVE, LAKE WALDEN, CONCORD, MASS.   COPYRIGHT, 1908, BY DETROIT PUBLISHING CO.

Considered the birthplace of the conservation movement, Walden Pond has been designated a National Historic Landmark.

Since Thoreau's death, Walden Pond has attracted those on self-imposed pilgrimages and those seeking artistic inspiration. They have built, stone by stone, the monument or cairn. Many of the stones are marked with dates and initials.

Thoreau's cairn

Thoreau had three chairs in his Walden house: "One for solitude, two for friendship, three for society."

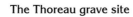

Thoreau's Home at Lake Walden

The Thoreau grave site

Quotes from Henry David Thoreau

A man is rich in proportion to the number of things he can afford to let alone.

Do not be too moral. You may cheat yourself out of much life. Aim above morality. Be not simply good; be good for something.

In wildness is the preservation of the world.

It is never too late to give up your prejudices.

Live each season as it passes; breathe the air, drink the drink, taste the fruit, and resign yourself to the influences of each.

Men are born to succeed, not fail.

Many go fishing all their lives without knowing that it is not fish they are after.

Our life is frittered away by detail. Simplify, simplify.

BRONSON ALCOTT AT ORCHARD HOUSE, CONCORD, MASSACHUSETTS

When Alcott bought the house, it stood in 12 acres of apple orchards, thereby the name: "The Orchard House."

Amos Bronson Alcott was unique in the way he embodied and lived out his transcendentalist ideas. As an educator, he believed that all knowledge and moral guidance springs from inner sources and it is the teacher's role to help these unfold in a beneficial way.

Alcott, a progressive educator, purchased two c. 1700 houses for his wife and four daughters. Moving the small house, he joined it to the rear of the main structure, making many improvements to the main house, known as Orchard House. Since then, no major structural changes have occurred. The rooms today appear much as they did when the family lived there.

In 1868, Louisa May Alcott wrote Little Women at a "shelf" desk built by her father and set the novel in this home.

Orchard or Alcott House, "Home of Louisa Alcott and her Little Women", Concord, Mass.

PARLOR, ORCHARD HOUSE, CONCORD, MASS.

LOUISA M. ALCOTT'S ROOM, ORCHARD HOUSE, CONCORD, MASS.

Children's Nursery, Alcott House, Concord, Mass.

Home to the Alcott family from 1858-1877, Orchard House was the house described in *Little Women*.

DINING ROOM, ORCHARD HOUSE, CONCORD, MASS.

IN LOUISA M. ALCOTT'S ROOM, "ORCHARD HOUSE", CONCORD, MASS.

THE STUDY, ORCHARD HOUSE, CONCORD, MASS.

THE STUDY, ORCHARD HOUSE, CONCORD, MASS.

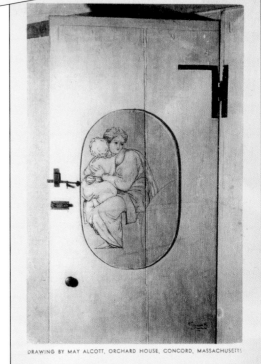

DRAWING BY MAY ALCOTT, ORCHARD HOUSE, CONCORD, MASSACHUSETTS

Quotes from Louise May Alcott

It takes people a long time to learn the difference between talent and genius, especially ambitious young men and women.

I put in my list all the busy, useful independent spinsters I know, for liberty is a better husband than love to many of us.

Now I am beginning to live a little and feel less like a sick oyster at low tide.

I'm not afraid of storms, for I'm learning how to sail my ship.

Louisa May Alcott. *Courtesy of Minute Man National Historical Park Museum Collection: MIMA 13731*

From 1859 to 1864, Amos Bronson Alcott served as the Superintendent of Schools in Concord. During his tenure, he founded one of the first adult education centers in the United States, The Concord Summer School of Philosophy, which stands to the left of Orchard House. By 1880, Bronson had constructed the building known as "Hillside Chapel" to house his school. For the following eight summers, this summer school introduced adults from throughout the country to some of the greatest thinkers of that period.

Concord, Mass. School of Philosophy.

PATH TO OLD SCHOOL OF PHILOSOPHY, WHERE CONCORD'S FAMOUS LITERARY MEN STUDIED, CONCORD, MASS.

MR. ALCOTT IN THE DOOR OF
THE SCHOOL OF PHILOSOPHY
Orchard House
Concord, Massachusetts

The Concord School of Philosophy

The Wayside House was originally the home of Samuel Whitney, muster master of the Concord Minute Men. During the events leading to the Battle of the Bridge, Whitney was with his company while Mrs. Whitney and her children watched the British march by the house on their way to search for contraband in the town.

During the literary renaissance of the nineteenth century, it became home to three families of authors. First, it was the home of Bronson Alcott, his family and his famous daughter Louisa May. Later Nathaniel Hawthorne and his wife lived there. He wrote *Tanglewood Tales* in this house.

Near the end of the century, the Lothrops purchased it. Mrs. Lothrop had already written *The Five Little Peppers and How They Grew* under the pen name of Margaret Sidney. A prolific writer, Harriet Lothrop helped preserve four historic sites in Concord: the Wayside, the Orchard House, the Grapevine Cottage, and the "Old Chapter House," also known as the Pellett-Barrett House.

The literary inhabitants of The Wayside have left many mementoes behind. The Wayside now belongs to the National Park Service.

Wayside, Hawthorne's home. Hawthorne made some substantive changes, including the so-called tower. The top floor of this three-story addition provided him with a study.

The older woman is Harriet Lothrop aka Margaret Sidney. *Courtesy of Minute Man National Historical Park Museum Collection: MIMA 13754*

Other Famous Concord Spots

Sleepy Hollow Cemetery contains Author's Ridge, with graves of many Concord notables, including Thoreau, Emerson, Hawthorne, Alcott, and Lothrop. It also has the beautiful Melvin Memorial sculpted by Daniel Chester French in 1906-1908 for three brothers who died in the Civil War.

2087. - PATH TO SLEEPY HOLLOW, CONCORD, MASS.

MELVIN MEMORIAL--SLEEPY HOLLOW CEMETERY, CONCORD, MASS.

Sleepy Hollow is quietly romantic.

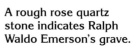

A rough rose quartz stone indicates Ralph Waldo Emerson's grave.

GRAVE OF RALPH WALDO EMERSON, CONCORD, MASS.

HAWTHORNE'S GRAVE, CONCORD, MASS.   2225

Hawthorne's grave is marked only with his name.

Grapevine Cottage was the home of Ephraim Bull, the developer of the Concord grape. Born in Boston in 1806, young Ephraim cultivated wild, native grapes and other fruits in his garden. Later he purchased seventeen acres of land near Concord and began growing grapes. Located on the Lexington Road, just east of the home of Nathaniel Hawthorne, Bull's farmhouse is still standing. More importantly, its garden still has the original parent vine of all the Concord grapes in the world. In 1853, the new seedling was exhibited before the Massachusetts Horticultural Society; in 1854, Bull placed the grapes on the market, calling them the "Concord Grape." The success of the grape was immediate, and in a few years the Concord grape had spread from Massachusetts to the Mississippi.

Ephraim Bull in his vineyard. *Courtesy of Minute Man National Historical Park Museum Collection: MIMA 14020*

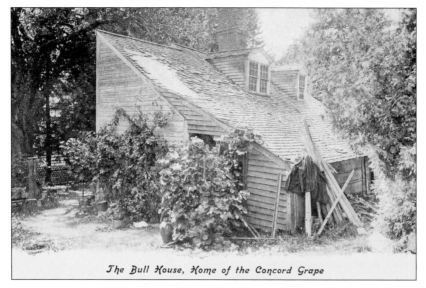

The Bull House, Home of the Concord Grape

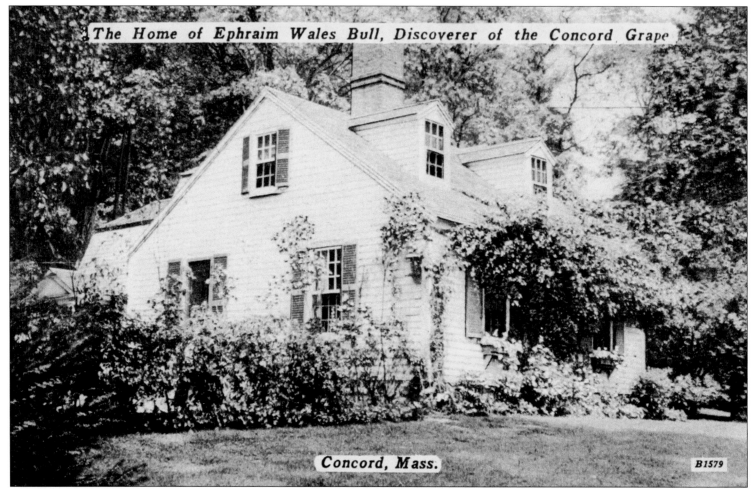

The Home of Ephraim Wales Bull, Discoverer of the Concord Grape

Concord, Mass.

B1579

126